# Finding the Line

## ordinary encounters in nature's mirror

### Brenda Peddigrew

iUniverse, Inc.
Bloomington

# Finding the Line
## ordinary encounters in nature's mirror

*(cover photo by the author: Little Kennisis River, Algonquin Highlands, ON, Canada)*

*iUniverse books may be ordered through booksellers or by contacting:*

*iUniverse*
*1663 Liberty Drive*
*Bloomington, IN 47403*
*www.iuniverse.com*
*1-800-Authors (1-800-288-4677)*

*Because of the dynamic nature of the Internet, any Web addresses or links contained in this book may have changed since publication and may no longer be valid.*

*Any people depicted in stock imagery provided by Thinkstock are models, and such images are being used for illustrative purposes only.*

*Certain stock imagery © Thinkstock.*

*ISBN: 978-1-4502-7765-5 (sc)*
*ISBN: 978-1-4502-7766-2 (ebk)*

*Printed in the United States of America*

*iUniverse rev. date: 12/17/2010*

*A certain philosopher questioned the holy Anthony. "How," said he, "dost thou content thyself, Father, who art denied the comfort of books?" He answered, "My book, philosopher, is the nature of created things, and as often as I have a mind to read the words of God, it is at my hand."* (quoted in Simon Small: From the Bottom of the Pond: the forgotten art of experiencing God in the depths of the present moment.)

*Believe one who knows: You will find something greater in woods than in books. Trees and stones will teach you that which you can never learn from masters.* (personal letter, St. Bernard of Clairvaux, 106:107)

*But ask now the animals, and they will teach you; and birds of the air, and they will tell you: or speak to the earth and it will teach you; and the fishes of the sea will declare themselves to you. It is the hand of God who made all this…*(Job 12:7-9)

*Every moment instructs, and every object: for wisdom is infused into every form. It has been poured into us, as blood; it convulsed us, as pain; it slid into us, as pleasure; it enveloped us in dull, melancholy days. or in days of cheerful labor; we did not guess its essence, until after a long time.* (Ralph Waldo Emerson: "Nature")

# Author's Preface

When I was about two and a half years old, my father took me fishing with him for the first time. I remember impressions of the quiet woods, the ripples and eddies of water, and most of all the big rainbow trout that came slapping in the air to where I stood enthralled by the whole scene. My father taught me to thread worms onto a hook, and he encouraged me to feel the fins and behold the colors of the rainbow trout; then he showed me how to clean it and prepare it for supper that night. In that early memory, my belonging to the natural world in all its expressions – silence, death, beauty of surroundings and touch, was forever wedded to being with my young, quiet father in his best presence.

I am mainly a poet, not an essayist, but when the *Highland Communicator*, a tiny bi-weekly paper in the Haliburton Highlands of Ontario, Canada (where I live) invited short pieces about local topics, I felt an urge to try it. I was already exploring the daily details of living on a river in a forest, so how better to share those experiences and the insights they evoked in me?

Thus began nearly four years of sending in an essay almost every two weeks. These are the essays in this book, with a few more added and some others that were published elsewhere. Those who waited for these essays every two weeks will be pleased that there are also a few extra in the same familiar mode of encountering some natural presence and allowing it to evoke a human life application, as I had unknowingly originally done on that day with my father.

Every one of the moments described here were numinous and revelatory. Through the privilege of writing these pieces and having them read, I found myself expanded and blessed with a comprehension of the natural world that would never else have happened. Through them my own humanity was deepened, and I understand my place in the universe better for having allowed these moments to sink into my momentary being, and then give them expression.

Through these simple and immediate reflections, may you too enter into these holograms of all life. Even without knowing Old Mill Road or the Little Kennisis River or the Algonquin Highlands, I hope they will take you into your own connection with the magnificent, present, world around us all.

The pages before you have many blank spaces. You are encouraged to fill them with your own sketches, quotes and notes.

*Brenda Peddigrew*
*SoulWinds, Algonquin Highlands*
*September 2010*

# Dedication

For my Father, who taught me to love the woods and the ponds and the trails and the animals of Newfoundland's Avalon Peninsula long before I could speak; and for JW, who lives that love in my presence, every day.

# Animals Know

One morning a few weeks ago, in deer-hunting season, I was walking my usual quick pace along Old Mill Road with our Golden Retriever Kai. At long last she has adjusted her walking to a consistent pace, without the abundance of pulling and sniffing that used to characterize these walks, though I'm glad to stop sometimes and let her follow her very sensitive nose. We've reached an excellent compromise on these morning walks.

As we turned a small corner on our way to the park, I saw ahead of us at some distance a deer, standing still as a carving, right in the middle of the road. She was staring straight at us, and Kai – in her new-found containment – didn't strain at the leash or try to run in her direction. The two of us just continued walking toward the deer at our usual pace, without rushing or making a fuss. When we about twenty feet away, the deer turned and leaped back into the marsh from which she'd come, though in no great hurry.

When Kai and I reached the spot where the deer had been standing, I saw on the ground something that shocked me with sudden violence. There on the ground was the bottom part of another deer's leg, from hoof to knee joint, with about eight inches of skin above the joint flopping empty when I picked it up.

I am vigilant about anthropomorphizing animals – another human arrogance- but I couldn't shake from my mind that morning the certainty that the deer was standing by a body-part of an animal she knew, perhaps a family member, and that she was bringing it to our attention. Kai didn't try to touch it or gnaw on it – also unusual – but

1

waited quietly while I picked it up and placed it with care in a little hollow in the earth to the side of the road, out of sight. I blessed the deer to whom it had belonged, and the one who'd been standing by it. I asked also for blessing on whomever or whatever had destroyed the body of this exquisite creature.

Kai and I walked on, more wrapped together than before. I felt myself to be in the presence of some layer of animal knowing that is hard to describe. I felt as if I'd received a gift. I felt suspended in another kind of time than I was used to. And I felt grateful that I am surrounded by animals, both wild and domestic, whose presence amplifies and enriches my own small understanding of this complex world. I want to spend a lot more time outside seeing and allowing myself to be seen – by trees, by animals, by all the myriad manifestations of the emerging natural world.

Animals know something I am only beginning to glimpse, in moments and soft encounters, breaking in on my schedules and the way I would like things to be.


Animals know.

## Animals Know (2)

When I wrote "Animals Know (1)", I was reflecting on the peculiar indications of knowing on the part of wild animals. It is a sense of some deep and large, a wordless resonance with something that we as humans are sometimes lucky enough to glimpse, if we pay attention in the moment of encounter.

With more frequency than wild animal encounters, we can experience this knowing when we pay attention to the communications of our domestic animals. Not only dogs and cats, but birds, rabbits, turtles – even fish communicate with us if we are focusing on them in the moment.

I have seen a cockatoo expressly choose his owner to nuzzle and cuddle: then lead her to his food to communicate his need in that moment. I have seen horses do everything but speak words, so clear is their communication of acceptance – or disdain – of people standing near them. In one instance of standing in quiet communication with two horses pulling a sled for hired rides, and while everyone else was greeting and talking before getting on board, I was shocked with the strong degree of sadness that I felt from those horses, that I saw in their eyes. I had to hold myself there, so moved was I by their helplessness. Then there was my encounter with a python – but that's a separate and entirely unique story that needs its own telling.

Where I do experience animal knowing on a daily basis is in Kai, our Golden Retriever, and MaChree, our black and white, long-haired cat. Beyond the ordinary communications of demanding food and asking to go out, or at least into the screened porch, there is a more subtle knowing on their parts that shows up when one of us receives distressing news, or is sick, or has company. Kai will come and lean against a leg if you are upset – sometimes knowing that before you do. MaChree will curl into a ball in your lap when you are sick, or even lie on the distressed part of your body. Sometimes either will ignore company; other times they will play raucously, distracting us from our attention to visitors. With this one we haven't worked out a pattern. But I have been known to speak loudly to MaChree in particular: "how can you tell me so much without words?" after I say to him "show me what you want; show me." And he does.

What is this mysterious strand of knowing that animals have and that we can open up to receive? I sometimes see it as a strand of light, linking us to the particular animal, a light along which travels wordless mutual communication.

All we have to do is be in the moment, and open ourselves to receiving, and trusting what they offer.

# Feast of Snow

Everyone knows what a feast is, and – no matter how many we have – a feast is universally welcome. In the Roman Catholic tradition, the word "feast" also refers to the special celebration of saints – days in which a particular person is remembered for doing or being an extraordinary expression of goodness in his or her particular time and place. But a feast of snow? In this winter, when it has hardly stopped coming down for months? What crazy person would even think of such a thing?

Well, I've been thinking of it, and fairly often during the past few months. I began to think of it in early December, after we'd been having snow for about a month. Walking along Old Mill Road one morning, I saw clearly the beauty of the whitely-draped forest, every tiny twig outlined in black and white. I was stunned for a few moments, and had to stop walking. I saw the ground drifts, elegant and graceful as sand dunes. I heard the crunching of my boots when I made the slightest move, and nothing else but the thick and comforting silence. That morning, though I have lost it often since, I felt imprinted with the winter's beauty, and it has mostly carried me through the trials and traumas that have also been true of this harsh season.

This early initiation into snow's demanding presence has caused me to go even deeper to find ways to be balanced in how I experience winter. I have learned to pause often as I shovel and clear the paths around the house, and to find that beauty so easy to miss with feet and feet of snow to clear. I have become more aware of my body – of its capacities and its limits – and of the necessity of resting more and stretching more with the physical demands of this season. Eating more as a response to this extreme cold is no hardship!

The presence of snow – with its demands and its beauty – sends me deeper into all the possibilities which might color my response to it. There are moments that I look out and despair that it's snowing again. There are moments that I rage and can't lift the shovel one more time. There are moments when I wonder how I came to live so close to the elements, and what a gift I've been given. Snow calls out the full range – for me – of human response.

For snow is one of those elements over which we have very little real control, and in that reality I am reminded, again and again, that human life is all of that range of emotion, and that every part of it is beautiful. The purity and magnificence of snow is a physical manifestation of the truth of human life. And so I celebrate, as often as I can, a Feast of Snow.

# Acts of God

Two weeks ago I had occasion to make an early morning visit to the emergency department of one of our local hospitals, accompanying a friend who was in terrible and unexpected jaw pain. The doctor on call was unabashedly puzzled as to the nature of it, and when he had made a few observations as to what it could possibly be – mostly in the nature of sending us on to Peterborough that same morning – my friend asked what could cause such pain. "I have no idea," he said, "act of God."

His use of this phrase caused me to remember another way it is commonly used: in insurance policies to describe unpredictable disasters from weather. How strange, I thought, that only debilitating pain and destructive natural disasters would be ascribed to God in this way – whoever God may be for the variety of believers and non-believers in our society. Surely not all insurance companies and their policy-holders are believers – yet "act of God" still appears in official, legal documents.

I kept on pondering the phrase as I observed the beauty of this fall season in our quiet and privileged part of the world. The early morning mists were unsurpassed this year, enticing me out by 7 am some mornings to catch the sun burning them through, to witness the silent presences emerging as mists swirled over the still lakes and the whispering river. As the mists diminished, colors brilliant from sun and shining with water drops left behind by them blazed in three-dimensional clarity, so crystal sharp that I'd have to look away. Who could describe, photograph, or even paint the shades of scarlet and gold, the oranges and yellows, the bronzes and deep greens surrounding us with glory? Who could communicate the cleansing winds, the unexpected warmth we had, the joy of those dancing, misty waters?

So I found myself wondering how we ever came to apply the phrase "act of God" in one set of circumstances but not the other. How we as a society can say that God causes pain and destruction, but not beauty and peace. I am still wondering how that could ever have come about. But the discrepancy gave me this gift: of noticing, questioning, and making me more mindful of what language I would use to ascribe a cause to what I cannot explain to my own or another's satisfaction. And to definitely call the beauty of this season "an act of God."

# A Quality of Light

Have you noticed the difference in the light these past few months, with so little snow and the long overcast of November? There were days, it seems, of only grayness, of evening in the afternoon. Some days my eyes could hardly bear to look at it, and I found myself doing a lot of walking with eyes cast down, though there was no need to be careful of icy footing either.

We have been hearing for years now, about global warming, but the escalating mention of this phrase every time there is an unexpected weather system or a change in predictable pattern is deceiving. Even in our recorded history, which is miniscule in the long unfolding of history, there have been many such unexpected seasons. Perhaps it is more important to expand our short seeing into a longer view, than to be hooked by the escalating anxiety of media voices of doom, whether it be about global warming or the coming flu pandemic, which is now sliding almost daily into the evening news.

This is not to say that neither exists or neither will happen. It is more about where we choose to place our attention: on the things we can affect, or the things we cannot. Though we can definitely decide how we choose to live our own lives, our attitudes towards events and what we make priority for each day, we cannot decide the quality of weather-light, or what it might bring us. Yet the first also clearly affects the second.

I miss the light of the sun. I miss the snow – though admittedly I am also relieved and thankful for a winter (so far) of less worry about driving and going places without that added concern. I have noticed also – with alarm – that when I'm standing outside in the few hours of direct sun we have had, the warmth is more like a March sun than a January one. I feel it on my back, warming me. I also notice with worry that some bushes have spring buds unfolding, and that green patches are visible in parts of the wet ground.

The alarm is important, because it causes me to be more attentive to what is actually happening with the planet, how her predictability is changing in ways we can actually track in our lifetime. But it also confronts me with a kind of human arrogance that I am very frequently guilty of: do we really think we CAN destroy this planet? The escalation around us of thinking we can actually do so has pushed me to a different thought: that she is, after all, with so many disturbances and disasters, really making her own adjustments, taking care of her own being, and survives with or without us.

The absence of light in this season has alerted me to how I take for granted the consistency of seasons, which perhaps has never been true. What does it say to you?

# Bear-ing It

When neighbors began to talk about having their bird-feeders smashed by black bears early in spring, it was the bears who had my sympathy. How would you like it, I thought (silently, I should add) if you drove to the IGA or Value Mart in Minden one day and there was an electrified wire fence around your main food source?

The fear of black bears has been fascinating to me for many years. Their size, color and penchant for human food seems to have evoked terror, that – taken in the context of other statistics we are given - is disproportionate in the extreme. One or two bear incidents in a season compared to the number of car accidents, drownings or reckless snowmobile or ATV drivers seems outlandish, if not hysterical, if you bring reason to the picture. Walking down Old Mill Road every morning in every season, I feel more threatened by drivers doing 60 or 70 kms on that curving, quiet road than I do by meeting bears there, which also happens regularly in three seasons.

Being paddlers, campers and hikers, educating ourselves about bears seems only reasonable in the midst of this conditioned cultural fear. What I learned about them from a man who established the "Walking With Bears" program in Northern Michigan – his life's work being to help people dispel their fear of black bears – gave me a reassurance I haven't lost. Hearing that bears have their own rules of courtesy which humans mainly violate out of ignorance, or choose to disregard, allowed me to realize that we are not encountering dumb animals here, but a culture all its own. It seems important to respect that, since we are living with them here, and in fact have taken over their land. In human language, they were here first.

The other most important thing I learned is that bears are more afraid of us than we are of them., and why would they not be, given how we treat them? This allows me to keep my own fear in check in their presence. Like all animals – dogs being our most common example – they smell our fear, and then sense that there must be something to be afraid of, so they make a bluster in the face of that, confronting the fear in front of them – us. Trusting this has allowed me, on many occasions, to shout "go home, go on now" while waving my arms and keeping my own fear in check when I meet them on the road - and they do: saunter or run into the woods. This has worked over and over even with mothers and cubs.

This is not to say that I don't also respect bears, and all other animals. Like us, they can be unpredictable, but not as often as humans. I won't do anything to taunt or tease them, or put myself in any danger from a rogue bear. Proportionately, however, humans are way more dangerous to humans than bears are.

We have invaded the habitat of bears and other animals. We destroy their food chain, remove their natural food sources. And now – after generations of training them to find their food at landfill sites – we suddenly remove that as well. Something is seriously missing from how we humans understand our place in this delicate, mysterious chain of being, and it could be something that will destroy us, sooner or later, if we don't wake up soon.

Perhaps we are mindlessly buying into the culture of alarm and fear that is escalating in our world. I would rather live by the title of a new book by Julian Barnes which I just encountered: "Nothing to Be Frightened Of," and stand in awe at the mystery of living here, in the Highlands, just bear-ing it.

# *Enough*

How did it begin? It might have begun at the garage sale that was necessary when we decided to move from Etobicoke to Halls Lake. The house here is nearly a thousand square feet smaller than the one there, so it was necessary to downsize the "stuff" that accumulates in a larger house, whether you intend it to or not. It was no hardship to divest ourselves. We were already more than excited about the house here, even being pleased about its smaller size.

Or it might have been an encounter with a friend of ours who had bought a high end digital camera a few months before. When we showed him ours, purchased just a few weeks before, he immediately said "oh, I don't have that feature or that one – I want your model."

That was the beginning of our consideration of the word "enough", but it didn't end there. As we arranged the rooms of our new place, there was a theme of "spaciousness" and "simplicity"; there was always a move towards less rather than more. Because we are both people who engage in a lot of projects, with a love of art and sculpture, keeping the space simple is an ongoing effort, but one that seems to have claimed us.

Finally we noticed what we were saying to one another and we began to talk about it. Someone had pointed out the phrase "less is more" in some article and though this is currently a popular aphorism for a particular group of people, we sensed that there was something amiss with it: what it really affirms, yet again, is the quest for "more" – that's the purpose of it, though now we get to "more" through "less".

Now we had it. We changed that aphorism to "less is enough", and we've been using it ever since. It helps us to notice when we are caught up with the pressure to buy new things, even when the old is still functioning well. It keeps before our eyes how manipulated we can be by advertisers always improving products and letting us know how much we need them. It constantly reminds us that our "enough" is riches untold in most areas of the world. And it frees us from that treadmill of always looking for something better, always rushing to improve, always giving precious time to shopping and searching for something new and better.

Realizing out loud that "less is enough" has slowed us down and kept us at home when we'd be otherwise haunting malls and stores. "Less is enough" has given us time to notice the beauty of where we live, and the calm that comes over us when we stroll slowly around the property, seeing that every season has its own attractions. "Enough" has stopped us from over-socializing, over-buying and over-indulging. Best of all, "enough" has given us time to be grateful and to know how privileged we are in this world where most are poor beyond our imagining.

# Finding the Line

I have been kayaking for three summers now, mostly on the Little Kennisis River that runs past our back door into Halls Lake. But it wasn't until this summer that I finally discovered – with the guidance of my housemate Joan – how to paddle easily back against the considerable current of a very high water release from the dam at the old log shute.

A few weeks ago, we woke up one Sunday morning to find the river empty. This had never happened before, and it was quite a shock. Later we heard that the dam had been illegally tampered with the night before, deliberately closed off altogether, and not by the MNR or the Trent Waterway personnel. Why this might have been so, beyond keeping lake levels higher, we couldn't imagine. So we were silenced by the sight of an empty river at our back door, and being opportunists, we took three hours to clear away the sticks and other debris we could usually never reach. Still, our first thought was for the fish and other wildlife that must have been affected that day. So we were thankful that – twenty-four hours later – the water was fully released, more than we'd ever seen it before. The current was very swift in its flowing.

Here's where kayaking comes in. Going downriver in that current was simply a matter of steering. It was a great ride and a quick one, but paddling back against it was something I'd never tried before. Following Joan, I heard again and again "find the line, find the line," meaning the finest diagonal direction across that rushing current. "Ferrying" is the correct term, I believe. After initial fumbling and over-exerting, I was astounded by how easy it was to paddle back, once I'd found the line.

The sensation of "finding the line" stayed with me for days. I found the phrase repeating itself inside, and taking on other applications. When I'm facing an overwhelmingly crowded day, for example, how do I find the inner line of slow, steady progress through all that must be done? When I'm facing disagreement and conflict, where is the line that holds me present without losing myself to a useless and destructive anger? And when I have to do something I'd rather not do but that needs doing, how do I find the line inside that allows me to do it? I couldn't help but remember that after learning the proper paddle move, it became easier, and perhaps the same could happen here.

The word "inside" is the key. "Finding the line" inside me, and remembering that it was a diagonal, not a straight line, seems important. Could a diagonal line allow me to flow with whatever happens, just as a straight line weds me to one way?

The poet David Whyte talks about "finding the one line already written inside you." That's the shimmering line of power and peace that allows us to face any current at all.

# Living in Two Times

As I walked down the techni-colored Old Mill Road one recent morning, I noticed that my mind was occupied with a number of things that had nothing at all to do with the walk or the road. Planning for work, what so-and-so had said yesterday, how I would handle a potential conflict – these all raced around in y head like bumper cars on a circular track. Then I saw the mists rising through scarlet and gold, and I dropped out of head-time.

For the rest of that walk, I noticed the yellowing milkweed getting its seed pods ready, and a warbler's song when it stopped on a branch on its long journey, and the stately reassuring bulrushes like marshy sentinels. I felt the sun dispersing the mists and how something cold inside me dispersed with the sun's warmth also. I saw a brown hare standing still as a statue not 10 feet from where I passed, and a shuffling groundhog crossing the road a hundred feet ahead of me. I smelled the pine and balsam fir, wafting on some still-warm air currents.

Suddenly, in the midst of that heavenly quiet, I realized that time and the concerns of time had drifted away. The fullness of now – and all that it opened out into – was all, all that filled me. I was just one other of Nature's cyclical presences, privileged to witness the ordinary community, to really see it, that first community to claim me as its own. I was born from the earth and into her body I would return. There was a joy and peace, a sense of rightness, with this thought.

The vast and infinite time of that walk shifted back in less than a second when I arrived back home. I had mistakenly recorded the wrong time for one of my clients to see me, and he was waiting in the garden, pacing. Time squeezed back like an accordion, and the minuteness of appointment times, meal times, work time, sleep time crowded out the timelessness of the morning walk.

What that morning taught me, by such sharp and sudden contrast, was that I live in two times, and – I suspect – so do we all: the expansive, timeless time of the present moment, and the contracted, small and tight time of interacting with the world that is necessary for function and task. Each is as important as the other, and if I spend too much time in one – contracted time, for example – I'm likely to become tight and small in my own view of the world. It's then that I go out, into the wide beauty of the natural world, and offer myself for its transforming, so as not to get lost.

Every day I try to live deliberately in two times.

# Nature's Adversity

Not many living in Haliburton County and the Alquonquin Highlands would argue that this winter has indeed demonstrated the adversity that nature can throw at human beings, focused as we are on comfort and security. Snow we can't keep up with clearing, winds that destroy not only trees, but property, rain that floods the most carefully built basement and swells rivers into forces of destruction – these have been our winter thus far. With all our machines, heating wires, and ergonomic shovels, snow has lost much of its reputation as a source of recreation, this winter.

But there is another side to this challenge, were we to cultivate the frame of mind that would see a different possibility. I realized it when I found myself writing to a friend who had expressed concern for the harshness of the winter that "it is making amazons of us!" And in writing that statement, I realized that this winter is bringing out a new strength, more than I perhaps would have credited myself with before now. Oh yes, I have griped and complained , and resented that so much time has to be given to clearing paths and roofs, to deciding visits based on weather alone, and to submitting other plans to weather approval. But it has also shown me how much I'm capable of doing – something I wouldn't have known without the adversity with which it is necessary to engage, this winter. I am stronger – physically and mentally – than I realized. Nice gift.

Suddenly this realization led me down a different but related path. I became aware of how clearly my whole life was shaped – not just by approval and achievement, but by resistance and even failure. The people who made it difficult for me throughout my life – and we all have them – actually sent me in a direction more of my own choosing than those whose approval I wanted and tended to please. They made it possible for me to stand alone and choose what was most congruent for myself in ways difficult to explain or justify to others, and – like this winter's weather – made me stronger than I'd be without them. I recalled the poet David Whyte's words: "if you can explain your chosen path to people in ways they can fully understand, then it's not your path."

So this morning, after another two hours of clearing snow, I have surrendered my resentment and opened a new mind-window. I can see now how adversity makes me stronger, whether it be snow or tornadoes or people. As always, nature is the mirror, waiting silently and without expectation always, for eyes to open and lessons to be perceived.

# Night Sounds

When I heard the big splash in the river not twenty yards from the screened porch where I was sitting, soaking in the silence of the almost-dark, all my senses came to life.

I had been doing nothing – at least what most people would call doing nothing – for nearly two hours. Just sitting in the porch at the end of the house, watching warm gold light transform itself into deep purple and then indigo. Full darkness would not arrive for a couple of hours yet.

It was a windless evening, and the stillness was seductive – and restful. I drifted into a lullaby place, being soothed by a variety of birdsongs, some of which I could identify: At one point, pushed by my continuously working mind, I actually found myself counting the names I knew…how beside the point. Listening was all that was needed for the music of the White-Throated Sparrow, the Ruby-Crowned Kinglet, the raucous Crow and the teasing Raven, the Chickadee and the screeching Heron. The Pileated Woodpecker and the Merlin Falcon pierced the quiet. Frog song filled the air with almost visible presences. Then woods crackled with footsteps and two white-tailed deer emerged into view, coming so close to the screen that I could distinguish the hairs on their faces and the silk of alert, standing ears.

Still – with all the sound and movement, the deeper forest silence did not seem disturbed. Until the splash. The adrenalin of fear seeped into my bloodstream and a high alert made me stand up immediately and peer into the nearly dark woods in its direction. The domestic animals with me in the porch – Kai the dog and MaChree the cat, who had hardly stirred at the deer, stood up with me at the large splashing sound.

Crashing and rustling of dry ground-leaves accompanied the dim shape of a large black bear. This was the rambling male that we had seen in the neighborhood twice this spring. He lumbered toward us, big sides shaking, and – despite my instinctive anxiety, I found myself thinking "what a beauty," and "how magnificent!" Then Kai began loud and indignant barking and I shouted as loud as I could – this was what I'd been told to do -and away he turned and ran in the direction of the landfill.

We sat again, the three of us, but the peace was disturbed. It took awhile for my blood and the animals to settle. I waited until the fireflies emerged in their numbers, and until the only sounds was the buzz of that orgasmic rhythm of light appearing like stars in the soft, silent night, making a fizzing sound as they touched the screen.

But what came to me in the restored silence was this: it was my own fear, and not the bear, that disturbed the peace of that spectacular and splendid evening.

# Pursuing Silence

Despite living among hectares of forests within which silence is profound, and highlighted – not broken – by multiple bird sounds, being silent for any length of time is impossible.

This was the thread of my thinking as I stood under the ancestral white pine that stands between the river and our house. I often stand or sit beside that tree, intuiting that it holds a secret of some kind, a secret that I want to know. It's the secret of stillness, and the secret of the peaceful ability to wait in silence.

Oh, I know I'm not a tree. But it's the quality of the tree's stillness – a solid, consistent, faithful presence – that I would like to experience now and then. I believe it would be a better contribution to the world than the rushing-around activity that I so easily fall into.

But silence is not so easily attained. Living surrounded by it outside – aside from the occasional chain saw, lawn mower, snow-blower, road plow or gunshots in hunting season – doesn't at all guarantee inner silence, where the gold is. In fact, the opposite is more often true: to place yourself in outer silence, whether it be in wilderness or simply turning off the electrical noises in your house, often amplifies the noise inside yourself. This is the reason why most people fear silence and do all they can to avoid it.

Why am I pursuing silence then? Why would anyone? There might be different reasons, but for me it's because this is the only way I hear my own inner voice. Only in silence do I know my deepest core, the place I call my soul. When I can drop below the crowded, unstoppable flow of thoughts I catch a glimpse of how much more there is to me than those

23

thoughts. I come closer to who I am and farther away from a mindless conformity to what is expected of me by a frantic, unreflective, noisy, cultural conditioning.

I have known glimpses of that inner silence. I have dipped into its rich vein of creative flow, feeling linked to the large energy of earth, of universe. In those moments, I am fully present to what is, and in that presence my tendency to split attention (affectionately called "multi-tasking") is momentarily healed.

Lately, my hunger for this silence is growing, and I am pursuing it. Doing so initiates a difficult struggle of letting go of worries, meeting deadlines, completing tasks – all of which are waiting and get done anyway – or don't. The world doesn't end. Much of it doesn't matter as intensely as my deceptive mind tries to have me believe.

What does matter is dropping into an inner silence, fully present, fully alive. What matters is that moment of experiencing the living bond that links us all, of feeling that oneness. All the struggle, all the pursuit, is worth that realization.

Standing below (and I might say "with" the ancient White Pine, as still as the river is moving, I am both – moving and still. I hear my own voice saying "this is what goes on."

That is all I need to know.

# SLOW

Walking along the snowmobile track that begins the Five Viewpoints Hiking Trail, eyes looking down to find the best placement for my skis on the rutted path, I suddenly look up to see, just at eye-level on my right, a yellow sign with black lettering: SLOW. No symbol, just the word SLOW.

Shocked for the moment, I fumble inside, thinking that the word is placed there just for me. It takes a few seconds to remember that it's for snowmobiles in winter and ATV's in summer. Because right now, in this moment, I know it's a direct message to my escalating life.

Standing there in the thick silence of a fading, golden light, on a weekday when most people are working at something that doesn't allow them to be here standing in front of a sign that says SLOW, I allow myself to fall into the chasm that this word opens in me.

I recall the swirling activity that takes over lives – mine and so many others who tell me that this is how it is for them. I feel the mindlessness that is the state brought about by constant moving and doing, the automatic pilot, the breathless ending to days with no pauses, no rest. No stepping into a space larger than our own immediate personal concerns.

Our culture conditions us to believe in constant, mindless activity as the "way things are", just as it does in constantly buying more and better things. It is George Bush, telling ordinary U.S. citizens that the best response they could make to 9/11 was to shop! Standing here in these silent, harmonious woods, I ask myself how far we are from that as Canadians. I don't like the answer.

25

The soft and startling moment of coming face to face with the sign in the woods fills me with a knowing that thinking couldn't do. I know how out of rhythm we are with earth's rhythms, how our inventions, especially artificial light, have alienated us from the ebb and flow that would make us healthy. I know how our ability to genetically modify food so that we can eat foods out of season with our bio-regions has removed us from the necessity of knowing ourselves made from the same soil. And I know how women's cycles, so resonant with moon and tide and a source of inner empowerment, have now become a nuisance, even a curse, the "illness" of PMS, requiring medication.

All of this rises to my awareness, standing here in the ebbing light of a snowy winter afternoon, confronted by a sign saying SLOW. Everything in me wants to walk on, pass it by and let the thoughts it has evoked fall away. But I won't. Some small, still part of me recognizes the gift of this startling, simple word SLOW. I savor it. Something in me sighs relief.

# Soul of Persistence

Until we moved to SoulWinds, I don't recall being concerned about black ants. But in our first two or three years here, every spring for bout a month they arrived with their quick black steps on counter-tops and cupboards, prompting a rushed trip to Home Hardware or Carnarvon Lumber for traps. Then I discovered Ant-Bi-Gon (yes, it's really called that), a harmless-to-animals powder that creates a chalky barrier along the edge of the house and across which ants' legs can't navigate.

So for the past two years we've been free of ants, except for the tiniest variety now and then. However, I often notice their tiny volcanic holes arising in the ground close to the house and always run for the powder to pour right in. The holes have gotten further and further from the house as a result, and of a distance that is no longer a nuisance to us. Neither do I want to kill them.

But recently, walking down Old Mill Road one bright morning, I began to notice the same brown miniscule volcanic holes in the pavement. It cannot be, I thought – they're not even near houses. But there they are, finding the slightest crack in the pavement, I suppose, and making large, round and slanted holes for their important work of coming and going and keeping the colony healthy.

There are many things to be said about ants that can be found with a quick google or library nature book, but the one I find most remarkable is their persistence. Block their way and they find another one. No energy wasted in complaining or fighting or arguing. A bit like water, actually – try to divert its course and it will just go round the obstacle.

Rivers always find a way through, even if it is to go underground for awhile.

I have begun to think that ants would be good models, even sacred creatures whose daunting powers might be worth emulating. Like cats for ancient Egyptians or cows for East Indian Hindus, we could well learn from the collaborative, dedicated and persistent nature of ants. Then we would never hear complaints of "what can one person do?" or "we're powerless to change the government – we're only ordinary people;" or "nothing to be done – the decision has been made."

Ants would never use that language. Knowing the limitless possibilities of life, they'd simply turn course and find another way. What would the world be like if we too, individually and together, treasured and cultivated the persistence of the soul's desire for light? For working for the common good? For the community as much as for the individual? We could do worse than look to ants. After all, it's nature that provides humans with all the models we need to get along on this earth, with ants being high up on that list.

# Burning Birch

Whenever I come to a log of birch in our woodpile, I'm already experiencing a little turning of joy, anticipating the several layers of pleasure I derive from burning birch.

First there is that extravagant bark, thick and layered, or thin and papery, extending over the sides of the split log like curly hair or new spring growth. I know that this is what will catch fire quickly...as will the log itself, dense wood giving fire to maple, oak hemlock and cherry long before some of them are ready. And the perfume of birch - I find it a richer fragrance than the most expensive manufactured perfume, for which my nose has no appreciation whatsoever. But if someone could bottle burning birch smoke, I would probably wear it.

Living in the forests of the Alquonquin Highlands allows me to know northern trees in a way I never would have otherwise. When I walk aimlessly in the woods with mindless attention – a practice I do far less often than would benefit my soul – I can now identify many varieties - white pine, red pine, hemlock, black spruce, white spruce, tamarack, balsam poplar, balsam fir, maple, northern red oak, black cherry, beech – and a few less common varieties – but it is birch that my eyes are drawn to, again and again. Yes, there is the beauty of it, but there is also something else, something more symbolic about birch that strikes a resonant chord deep inside me.

Birches shed their skins. Year after year, more noticeably around March or April, large sheets of birch bark imperceptibly leave the safety of the solid trunk of its stable tree. If you watch one tree every day for awhile, you will that this happens almost overnight in the warming of the March sun. Like human beings at the end of a long winter, it seems that the birch is saying "what a relief to get all these heavy clothes off!" and drops its bark to the ground.

Birches remind me of the many skins I have shed over the course of sixty –three years, and they are many. What's more, there are probably a few more to go before the final shedding of this body, the skin that life chose this time round. Birches confront me with this inescapable truth, one I turned away from for years and years. Now, as I grow closer to birch, as I honor its shedding and benefit from its particular warmth and scent and fire capacities, it has become yet another teacher. (In a similar way, I have become a friend of snakes, but that's a story for another day.)

In one of the healing stories about Jesus, he asks a blind man whose sight was just restored "what do you see?" The man replied, "I see people, but they are like trees walking." His restored vision might not have been so far off: I might have been a birch in another life, and faint echoes of birch-being continue to guide me through my human one. Birch shedding and birch burning seem little different from the stages and shedding of human life.

And what could be better than leaving behind a wafty, welcome, familiar scent as it/we pass from one state of being to another?

# The Birches' Voice

When winter is white, as it usually is, birch trees blend into the scenery so well that I hardly ever see them until the muddy brown of spring returns.

Because the first months of this winter were different, were without snow at all, I noticed on my daily walks that pure white color, almost glowing, whenever it appeared among the dun landscape. Yesterday morning it was an Arctic hare, standing perfectly statue-like, not five feet from the side of the road, smelling our smells and hoping not to be detected. And he wasn't, because we successfully distracted our prancing Golden Retriever from leaping in that direction. Another time it was it was the white streak of an ermine – the winter weasel – running along the dark river's edge. Do they know, I wonder, that they are not hidden this year?

But it is the birches that catch my attention the most urgently. In groups their arms splay out from the ground like arms trying to touch the heavens. When the infrequent sun is shining, they give off an actual light, as if responding to a request from some sovereign lord to show us humans a little faith in the possibility of brightness in this overcast winter.

More than all these, however, I notice the large rolls of bark that birches are sloughing off like the skins of snakes. Like most other living things, birches shed, dropping to the ground – usually around March – a material that gets recycled as firestarter, card and craft material, or food and shelter for small animals and insects we might never notice.

This year, the birches are speaking to me every time I go outside. Their voices, wrapped in light and the release of their protective skins – are not whispering as they do in snowy winters when they can hardly be seen. In this dull landscape they shout, they insist, they don't allow my eyes to skim over them or ignore them altogether. Instead, they throw questions at me like delicate inquisitors: "Where is your light and how is it being seen now?" they say. And "what is it you need to shed, loosen, get over and release so you can go on in the brightness of the life you've been given to live?"

There are many more ways to communicate than with words, as I often remark about (and to) my cat MaChree, who is one of the most effective communicators I know without using a single word. The birches are just as effective, throwing their wordless questions and shining statements into the winter air.

# Eye of the Birch

A few mornings ago I was sitting on the brown leafy ground of the overgrown woodlot on the south side of our house. I had discovered a small dip in the land, a comfortable hidden space surrounded by rotting stumps and green overgrowth. It was quiet there, the morning light patchworking the air. My breathing slowed and deepened, and I gathered the energies of the day before its distractions demanded most of my attention. In this sanctuary, the moment was all there was. Presence without thought.

Suddenly I became aware of a birch tree on the edge of my vision. When I turned to look, I was jolted by seeing that its bark was marked in such a way that it seemed to have eyes, and that those eyes were seeing me. I felt myself to be the focus of a benign attention, a compassionate grace.

Then the "being seen" amplified into a larger awareness, and I became conscious of how little we humans ever consider that – as we look at nature – nature is also looking at us. That we seldom think of this signals how strongly we think ourselves separate from nature, that we are its managers and users and mainly neglectful caretakers, but that we are somehow outside it, removed from it, above it. How then is it that our bodies are mostly water, that our lives begin as tadpoles swimming in search of a receptive egg, that we swim in salt water for nine months in a womb little different from a bear's or a groundhog's? And that – oh can this be true – when we die, our bodies turn back again into the good Mother, a rich humus of worms and soil, preparing to seed another expression of herself? "You are dust (soil) and unto dust (soil) you shall return" is perhaps the truest statement spoken.

The eye of the birch also reminds me that the stillness of animals is part of the seeing landscape, that they too are looking at us as we make our noisy way through their delicate habitat. I am realizing that the thought of being seen by them out of this stillness is somehow even more comforting than seeing them – this includes even the bear who was standing in contemplation by our back door the other night, just coming on dark.

Since that morning, I walk in nature very differently. Yes, when my small thoughts take over my mind, it matters little whether I'm in nature or on a busy street. But when I still that raucous crow of a mind, and open to receive the quiet, undemanding presence of tree and grass and every growing and dying thing surrounding me, I feel as if I truly am receiving something – a blessing. a word of encouragement, a reassurance that whatever I'm agitating about will pass. Nature has seen it all and is still here. More than that, I am carried on larger wings than my own and that is peace, however momentary. More and more, I settle into being seen in nature, rather than only seeing.

This is my gift from the eye of the birch.

# The Spring Shows

When I lived in Etobicoke, I waited eagerly throughout each winter for the spring shows, and often went to many of them: Cottage life, Sportsmen, Outdoor Life, Canada Blooms…you get the picture. Somehow, though I really bought little, the shows confirmed for me that winter was over, and color came back into the world.

Since moving to Haliburton County, I've not attended a single one of those "spring shows." instead, I am brought to a standstill each day by the true "spring show:" earth's emergence from the death of winter.

What a clean sweep winter makes! Everything appears to die – "appears" being the key word. And how do things live in that deadly, paralyzing cold? Yet, as soon as the sun – that mystical originator of all life on our planet – pushes out a bit more warmth – the whole earth responds by leaping out of the soil. Which is what happened this spring, with our early April heat.

This year the show is spectacular. Every one of my senses experiences some dancing with delight every day, and every day there's something new. I am almost blinded by the singular and particular appearance of so many distinct colors of green, and by the vivid colors of early blossoms that I'm sure I didn't notice last year. I stand paralyzed, hardly breathing, amidst hundreds of birdsongs that I am very slowly learning to name. I am more alive when I taste the new dandelion and the first fiddleheads, bursting with spring energy. When my gardener's fingers dig into the soil, warmed only at the top, and when I can be warm enough to allow the rain to fall on my skin without running for a coat, I feel the blessings. And then there are the smells! This year I am drunk with hyacinth and balsam poplar and other unnamable fragrances, and that musky pine smell that rises from the ground and seeps through the pores of my skin.

And I've said nothing yet about the birds who inhabit our river – herons and a pair of American Bitterns, Wood ducks and Black ducks and a snowy American Merganser couple and the two Canada Geese who nested on the river this year. There is the Broad-Tailed hawk and the tiny Merlin falcon chasing a raven from his territory. And besides birds we see beaver and muskrat and fox and weasel and otter, and – on Easter Sunday afternoon – fourteen Blandings turtles sunning on a log, not to mention the giant snapper who bumped the kayak of my housemate.

Oh, I am only just beginning to love the earth, as Denise Levertov (poet) said when she turned seventy. At least I have a few years on her. And every year, for the rest of whatever time I have left, I want to get to know – intimately, particularly, and erotically – the spring show that takes me into its boudoir and nourishes my every sense. And my soul too. Who would want to go to the International Center in Mississauga after that?

# The Hummingbird Show

During the summer, our television set gets a rest. We hardly think of it, except for the occasional news and weather. Instead, we are outside as much as possible, drawn by the subtle power of light and shadow, wind and stillness, bird sounds and wild animal visits. Watching the garden grow, the daily changes in vegetables and flowers somehow take on a magnetic quality in this season. And, of course, there is the ever-present flow of the river which flows by our back door, talking and singing and reflecting light in continuously changing patterns. There are days that we seriously believe we are living in paradise, and we stop and say "thank you" to whomever is listening.

This is not to say that we're without entertainment.

Most evenings now, beginning around 5 pm when the day begins to cool, and continuing into darkness, we stand in our garden for long periods and watch the hummingbird show. Beginning at the river we have a long swath of scarlet bergamot, otherwise called "bee balm," sweeping for over a hundred feet upwards towards the house. At this season, the bee balm grows over five feet high, many of them developing double crowns, giving them even more height. From a distance they resemble a river in themselves, red as bright blood. Edging the bee balm is tall mallow, bursting with multiple pink flowers and guarded by lines of black-eyed susans. This is where the hummingbird show – accompanied by the loud buzzing of hundreds of bees – is performed every evening.

A dozen or more hummingbirds – they're so fast that they're impossible to count – race and wheel among the bee balm, fighting for place and possession. They chase and jab one another; they drop and dive, then fight for height, one above the other. They drop into the bee balm and seem to hide until another finds them and claims the juicy prize they thought they had just a moment before. All of this takes place at speeds our eyes can hardly follow, and is accompanied by tiny screeches and protesting bleeps, a continuous cacophony of sounds that is somehow musical and discordant, all at once.

There is something mesmerizing about this show. We stand at the edge, silent observers, eyes darting around in an attempt to follow one or the other of the participants in the show. Bees come to check us out, fearing their own loss, and soon abandon our uninteresting bodies for succulent mallow. Stand there long enough, and you become part of the scene, we tell each other – and we do. We become part of the breathing of the earth who makes this glorious display of beauty and terror, all at once. We turn away reluctantly, alive in ways we weren't before. When darkness hides the hummingbirds, the show is over for us, but not for them, and we wonder what goes on when we're not there. But that's not our business.

When the cold of winter drives us indoors and back to more television for some of our entertainment, we are always aware of how superficial it is compared to our hummingbird show. How second-hand, how contrived it is, with shallow plots and forced caricatures of people. Alright for awhile, but it's the hummingbird show that catches the memory, and the imagination, dreaming us towards summer again.

# Seasonal Cleaning

When I woke this morning to go on my early walk along the Old Mill Road, the winds were raging. The sentinel white pine on the edge of the river outside the window was leaning from side to side with the force of it. Leaves were blowing like snow; yet, the temperature was easily that of a summer morning.

When I set out along the road, I didn't notice at first the amount of debris, lost in thought as I usually am before the sights and smells pull me out of my self-absorption. Then I began to see that the pavement was actually a pale orange rather than its usual dull grey, and that the pale orange was a covering of pine needles, blown right from the forest floor and off the trees onto the pavement! This went on for the whole of the walk. Then I saw small branches with leaf clusters actually being pulled from the trees and floating to the pavement. "Nature is doing her cleaning, today", was my first thought.

The change of seasons was being heralded by these winds, cleansing and moving everything around. Tomorrow is the fall equinox, the official end of summer, and the cleaning is timely; in fact, I recalled, Nature has ways of cleaning at the turn of every season. This morning's walk reminded me that we're coming into my favorite of all seasons: the long dark evenings,. the quiet preparing for winter, the lessening of social interactions until Christmas, and a more direct engagement with Nature herself through her weather. Autumn is my most creative time: as the light lessens, my inner creativity stirs in the dark and expresses itself with a fullness and variety that it doesn't have at any other time of year.

We too are expressions of Nature. Aren't our rhythms similar to hers, though we have lost touch with them through all the ways we disconnect and protect ourselves from her seasons? Yet, her seasons still move through us: emptying, stillness, sprouting, abundance. These rhythms move us even when we're not aware of them.

This morning's winds on the eve of the Autumn Equinox remind me that we too have a need to cleanse ourselves at the turning of the seasons. Many people put away summer things as a way of cleaning and caring for their houses and property. That's good, but it's not what I mean. There's an inner cleansing also needed, a stripping away of what is no longer needed inside – old grudges and attitudes, old ways of looking at the world that no longer serve us.

And perhaps we, like Nature herself, can let the Wind do it for us.

# The Hunger for Light

A few days after Hallowe'en I was driving east to Haliburton along Highway 118 in early evening when my eyes were drawn to approaching lights. I could hardly believe my eyes. They were Christmas lights, and it was only November 3. The whole house was outlined, as well as a big candle and several smaller Christmas forms. That very evening, the clocks were going back, giving us an extra hour as well as earlier dark evenings. Why were Christmas lights out so early? I wondered. It sent me careening into thinking about light.

This is my favorite time of year. I love the long, dark evenings. Over many years I've noticed that this is when I'm most creative, swirling with ideas and time to carry them out. Even when I'm busy, the ideas keep coming at this time of year. As darkness increases, I seem to be pulled deeper into a swirling cauldron of color and expression, as if the darkness were the source of it. I also love Christmas, and it's about our capacity to put light into darkness, and the colors that explode at this time of year.

But the woods and the rivers and the lakes...they stay in the darkness, moon and stars their only light. Trees lose all color, and walking in November offers high contrast from walking in October. On the other hand, a different quality of the woods becomes visible when all the leaves are gone. You can see farther; it has its own stark and spare beauty as the earth pulls all her life's blood inside against the cold.

What is it with us humans? I wonder. Are we addicted to light, afraid without it? Or perhaps it is that we make light just because we can, just because it gives us a sense of power, of being in charge. Are we still afraid of the dark? What about silence and stillness? Everyone might have a different answer to those questions, and there might be others I haven't even thought to ask.

The hunger for light is most evident at this time of year. Colors and shapes light up our darkness as at no other time. Might we be following the ancient instincts of ancestors, who never quite trusted that the sun would return? Might we be running from the original creative expression that darkness and stillness offer us? Or perhaps we simply (as I suspect is true for more of us than we think) love the shoots of joy that light in darkness evoke, even in the silly Santa shapes and cute angels and smiling snowmen. Deep in the darkness, light awaits, and deep in the light, darkness dwells. Without one, there is no other.

# Summer of Families

This is my fourth summer living at SoulWinds, but this is the first summer that I have seen so many new animal and bird families in their numbers. First there were the new goslings of the Canada Geese on the river, two parents and five babies, now four. A mother loon who first appeared with two babies now swims with one. A merganser mom travels Halls Lake with seventeen chicks, making considerable flutter when they suddenly and simultaneously beat their wings to go faster in the water.

One evening two weeks ago we were taking supper out into the screened porch when we noticed our cat MaChree perched on the back of a chair in his focused hunting pose, staring through the screen. When we looked with him, we saw a ruffed grouse with six small ones, all finding their way through the summer foliage at the back of the house. We forgot to breathe, so close were they and such a wondrous sight it was. Then, walking our dog Kai one morning last week, we noticed her particular attention on a spot at the side of the road between our house and that of our neighbor's. We stood very still, holding Kai leashed. A mother weasel emerged, looking around, and then gave some kind of signal to the six tiny ones waiting in the grasses. In some strange dignified manner, they all crossed the road together, scampering from danger.

Two mornings ago we were walking along Old Mill Road as usual when we noticed loud screeching sounds, the familiar voice of the Merlin Falcon whose territory this is. We hear the Merlin almost every day and once saw it chase ravens from its territory, unafraid of birds so much larger than itself. On this morning, however, there were at least three Merlin voices, and the others were very obviously young ones. Standing very still, we watched as the Merlin mother urged the young ones to fly from the nest-tree to one of equal height across the road. Two went over but seemed unwilling to come back, despite the parent's commanding cries. We waited until she flew over to them, all the way screeching impatiently. We thought we heard "Get back here now!"

All I can think of as I see these new families is the abundance and predictable renewal of the earth. I see the shining beginnings of life all around us, whether we notice it or not, all the time. I see the interdependence of all the species and how there's no such thing as a nuisance animal or bird, insect or plant. How difficult it is to look at the earth this way, and how necessary.

This summer of families reminds me of how extravagant earth is, how she prepares herself for loss, how she surrenders to unavoidable change. And how we as human beings have lost touch with her cycles and perhaps – as a result – with our own fertility. A fertile emptiness – the rest and renewal of creative powers – aligns us with the most powerful creative potential available in the universe. And that's why one square inch of the smallest eco-system on earth is worth more than all the computers, cameras, PDA's, MP3's and any other smart technology that will ever be invented.

# The Road's Bend

Every morning I walk the same way: from our house to Old Mill Road, which leads to Elvin Johnson Park and the causeway joining the Island in Halls Lake to the mainland. Usually Joan is with me, but not always, and our Golden Retriever Kai, who is always. Sometimes visiting friends want to go a different route, and I'll go with them, but I haven't been able to find the sense of belonging and connection that this daily, early morning route gives me. So I am pondering here as to why that might be.

First of all, it's the entrance to Old Mill Road that pulls me in. A few yards from this beginning, there's a bend, a small curve that doesn't allow me to see the rest of the road. There's a turning, and the thick trees appear to meet each across the road, just for a few seconds of the walk. This turning almost always, if I'm paying attention, awakens a jolt of possibility.

Here is where we were shocked speechless that morning in August after the tornadoes, at the sight of the whole road covered with fallen trees like matchsticks thrown carelessly in a pile. A deer was splayed beneath two of them. Here is where, with Kai's help, I found the wounded hare, and carried him home wrapped in my jacket. Here is where we watched a mother Merlin falcon teach her two babies to fly one morning last spring, our necks sore from watching the show. Here is where the bear frightened Kai, who was then lost for five days. The first bend of Old Mill Road is a place of mystery, of never knowing what the rest of the road might present at the beginning of a day.

But there are also other bends as we continue walking to the causeway. They too – often veiled in a mist that makes the trees seem to lean over and touch one another, creating a passageway through which we walk – become doors to the unknown, every morning. Sometimes we meet the Alquonquin Highlands caretakers in their truck, checking the park, and we stop for a chat. Or around the next bend is a new cottage being built. Often a hare, already in a noticeable white coat, sits in the middle of the road until Kai gets very close and then taunts her by leaping away, always just in time.

Such ordinary things on an ordinary morning, you might say. Yet I can't help but notice that a bend in a road behaves exactly like a bend in a day, a bend in my small-sighted plans when the unexpected presents itself and all that I thought would happen that day drops away in the blink of an eye, to emerge or not to emerge later. The road's bend is also life's bend, that large flow of time we turn away from except in an attempt to control it. The road's bend – that familiar turning in Old Mill Road – is as good as any for reminding me of this, every morning.

# Speed Bumps

In the season when bears roam the Highlands freely, many people – both cottagers and year-rounders – would readily name them as the greatest danger. I have written about this before in this column, and most readers know already where I stand on this topic – with the bears. Now I have come to notice what I believe is an even greater danger in the Highlands and that is speeding drivers.

Any evening on the local news you can see report after report f the fact that even outlandish fines are failing to slow down the ever escalating speed of Ontario drivers. In summer, that rush and hurry makes itself felt here, as people try to leave behind their pressured and over-filled lives – unsuccessfully. Instead, loud music at late hours, buzzing speedboats, and driving too fast on quiet country roads take over the rest-of-the-year pace for which many of us moved to the Highlands. The summer population swell is most important to the economy – that is not to be forgotten – but it also needs to be safe and manageable. Being regular walkers and mountain bikers, we have noticed this danger many times, and have mused again and again about how useless it is to post speed limits along these roads. Who, after all, would enforce them? Yet our country roads are narrow and winding, quiet and thick with green growth - and regularly spoiled by the threat of too-fast cars barreling along without thought of animals or walkers or bikers around the next unknown corner. Thus one morning on the walk we mused that a better answer to this problem might be speed bumps. Or – as one brighter friend proposed – don't fix the potholes!

Then it occurred to me that speed bumps are more evident in other ways as well. What if we adjusted our view of illness, for example, as a speed bump? What if we could see a sobering diagnosis of heart or thyroid disease, diabetes or diverticulitis or stomach ulcers or headaches or broken bones - not as illness, but as a speed bump, shaking us up into slowing us down?

For speed is the false god of our culture today. We worship it. We expect it. We strive for it. And if we can do five things at once with great speed, we'll be congratulated for it. The cultural addiction to speed, to instant everything, has subtly filled us with expectations, that – if not met – turns us into petulant children.

Our preference for getting through our daily list as quickly as possible has turned us into stones skipping over the water's surface and resenting/resisting the drop into depth that slows us down. But slowing down is something that will happen whether we choose it or not. Weather does it. Age is even more effective. Speed robs us of an inner life, and it severs us from nature, the Mother of all things coming slowly into their time and season.

So speed bumps, whether on the road or in the body or the soul, might be seen as invitations, at the least, or wake-up calls to notice what is really happening in this moment. An old Zen aphorism helps me:

"Muddy water, let stand, become clear."

What if obstacles were only meant to turn our heads in another direction? Speed bumps might not only slow us down, but open window after window into vistas previously unseen, or even thought about.

# Smelling the Wind

One morning in the late fall I stepped out into air and light still with that noticeable stillness of deep overcast. My cat MaChree, who takes me for a slow walk every morning – because of wild animals he doesn't go outside alone –led me to a small and sheltered circle of trees on our property, and there I stood in the stillness, he having found enough mouse-smell to keep him occupied.

While he was smelling mouse, I became suddenly alert to the smell of the wind, the slightest of movements in the air. It had the effect of bringing me to breathless attention: all my senses became engaged with this smell of wind. And what was this smell? It was of damp rain. It was of earth decayed. It had a hint of ice, the kind that slaps and stings your face. It was the smell of impending winter. All of this arrived on the wind in that one almost imperceptible stirring of air, which I would have missed altogether had I not been standing still, outside under trees, with my cat MaChree.

You might say "but what's the point? Go inside and stay warm and listen to the weather report!" And you would, of course, be right, be sensible, be very much in keeping with the comfort of modern conveniences.

But here is what you would be missing: your body alive with tingling connection; your senses wild with imagination, engaged all at once, breathing with everything around you. And in that one moment knowing that you are standing in a place that speaks to you in a language that doesn't use words, and that you are understanding what that language is saying.

Here in the Alquonquin Highlands, it's easy to go outside, to be among trees, to recognize the silence that relieves us from the steady and increasing noise of what is asked of us in contemporary life under the usual guise of "keeping up." But going out into that silence doesn't guarantee that you will smell the wind, or hear the birches, or see the pure white of the Arctic Hare standing perfectly still not five feet from the road. That takes emptying the mind, slowing the heart, and opening a space inside yourself that listens and waits.

Sometimes, it takes a slow walk with a cat to receive the gift of smelling the wind.

# The Zen of Tubing

We live on a river which invites tubers of all kinds during the summer season. People tube with children and dogs, pulling refreshments on ropes in the cool river water. They tube in the dark, disturbing the natural night quiet. The variety of this riverbed allows for all manner of tubing adventure. Those who want risk of injury to life and limb choose the high rapids. Those who want just a little bit of adventure go breathlessly over the smaller rocks, taking care to keep sensitive body parts above the tube's limits. After that there's what we call "the rocking chair", a gentle movement much resembling the name we have given it. Some of the adventure is the challenge of staying in the middle of the river so as not to get hooked or turned over by the branches and fallen trees along the sides, or by the eddies which frame the current, pulling the unwary tuber into a stillness not wanted on this particular ride.

Most of the river, however, is simply slow or fast, without rapids or rocks at all. It is also very shallow; in most places, not above the waist of an average adult. Floating from our dock to the lake takes an hour of very slow motion, unhindered by rocks or even many fallen trees, unlike the tube run in the river above where we live. There are also many turns, deep turns, in this river, and as the river approaches the lake, its current slows down, meeting the lake water towards which it was rushing when it was further away.

These two distinct parts of the river raise a question for me: which really is the greater challenge? Is it the rapids, providing excitement and some risk, raising the adrenaline and thereby providing the "rush" so appealing and so valued in our present way of living? Or is it the slowing down necessary in the lower part of the river, when speed is not a choice, and surrender to the river itself is the only option? (One could, of course, get up and walk to the side and out of the river, but we're not talking about that here.)

My own experience tells me that surrendering to the slowing current is the greater challenge. As the river gets slower and slower, my own rushing thought doesn't slow down at the same pace. I sometimes find myself paddling at the sides of the tube in order to make it go faster. I have to remind myself to surrender. I want to get to the end faster than the river wants me to. There is always a point in which this struggle becomes apparent, a point when the choice has to be consciously made. Making it changes me inside: I relax.

Letting the river take me instead of my taking the river is a choice so profound in its simplicity and implications that I have to slow down in order to think about it. What a lesson for life; what a challenge – to go against the grain of a culture that worships and lives by speed above all.

# Turtle Grace

As I came out to get into my car this morning, I missed something large and lumpy on the ground about ten feet from the car. In fact, I was already in, car started, when I saw her: a huge turtle, well over a foot long and several inches high. There she was, one foot pulled in, lying in the dry gravel, unmoving. I thought she was injured, and my first thought was to get her into water. All the while my mind was racing about how and why she might have gotten to this spot, behind our garage, so far from the river. Without waiting – and because I was on my way out, I must admit – I ran to get a shovel and with some difficulty slid it as gently as I could beneath her. She hardly stirred at first, but when I lifted the shovel she began to emit a long stream of water, which I took as an anxiety response. So as I struggled with the weight of her while making for the river, I spoke to her soothingly. As we came around the house and in sight of the river she extended her head and raised it, as if smelling the nearness of water. I rushed to let her slide in, and – indeed – her vitality was evident as she swam swiftly away.

It was only afterwards, talking about the turtle with my housemate, that we realized what the turtle might have been doing. Around the spot where she was lying were several digging marks. She might have been laying her eggs, or at least preparing a spot to lay them in. I might have interrupted her process. We are now uncertain as to whether any eggs actually lie in the gravel of the driveway, but we are protecting that spot until it becomes evident one way or another.

However the situation turns out, this brief encounter with a large turtle stopped my heart for a few moments and woke me up in a different way this morning. I realized yet again how I was living in my head and didn't even see her as I walked out to the car, so preoccupied was I with my busy thoughts that I wasn't present to my immediate surroundings. The turtle caused me to question what other things I might be missing if I continue this way. She also made me remember other associations: how First Nations peoples venerate turtle as the most ancient of all symbols for the earth as Mother and Goddess, and how for them North America is called "Turtle Island." Because of encountering this turtle I thought of "The Tortoise and the Hare" as I drove away, recalling its message that bigger, faster, louder doesn't win the day and that there are other ways to move through the world, slower ways that appeal to me more at this time of life. I recalled how sometimes I wished I had a turtle shell for protection, with her ability to pull inside when threatened or to snap when startled unawares. And I had sometimes thought of the fertility of turtle, how she lays dozens of eggs each year in the dry earth, and I wished to be as fertile as she is with ideas and with giving them solid ground.

In that few moments when the large turtle shocked me out of busy preoccupation of mind and heart, what I received from her was grace, and a definite awareness of my own organic nature, my link with the earth and all creatures of the earth. What grace indeed.

# Slipping Out of Time

I can't say about anyone else, but I have a real problem with time. The problem is not about feeling I have too little of it, though lots of people say that's their problem with time – no, mine is more about feeling the constraints of it. It's about schedules and deadlines, and the pressure that comes with them. It's about squeezing in too many things into too little time, or feeling I have enough time to do this, this and this, when I only have time for this. Relating to time in this way, which has haunted me for a lifetime, used to serve me well when I was teaching, traveling and facilitating, but now it feels too small, too tight, and I am straining at the boundaries that time sets up. I no longer want to be – literally – timebound.

A few days ago, in the warming spring weather that we have been having, I took out my bike and rode – reveling in the freedom and feeling ten years old again – to Halls Lake in the early evening to witness the sunset and to see how the ice was faring in all the warmth. There, sitting on a bench in the empty Elvin Johnson Park, I was wrapped in stillness and in the silence that only an early spring evening seems able to bring about. The cries of geese, ducks and gulls as they negotiated the edges of the remaining fragile ice highlighted rather than interrupted the silence. The light was silver, edged in gold, and it illuminated that familiar landscape in a way I'd not seen before.

My active mind tried its best. All the concerns of the day swirled and jumped around and tempted me into believing that something new could happen if I'd just listen to its repetitive rap song, a song of thoughts that really hadn't changed much all day. This is a familiar illusion, and I've made some small progress these past few years in dis-illusioning myself about that particular belief. But stream of inner thought is far from giving up, and as I sat surrounded by the stunning stillness around me, it tried again. I didn't want to listen. Perhaps it was that very definite decision – that I wanted a break from my own mind – that brought about, spontaneously, something that I've been practicing for awhile; i.e., dropping out of my thoughts into a deeper, calmer space that is simply being present without words, without naming, and being still. And – at this moment on the edge of Halls Lake on a new spring evening – I discovered that dropping out of the endless stream of thoughts meant also slipping out of time.

Sitting there, time passed without my knowing it. Without my checking my watch, without my wondering how long it would take me to get back, without enumerating what tasks I had left to do that evening. I felt dropped into a well of presence, a comforting sense of belonging to all I saw before me: the lake with its thin edges of ice, the light of silver and gold, the vibrant birds, the distant treeline, the sand on which my bench had survived the winter. There was no time involved. When I next looked, time had passed, but I had not noticed, not bothered about parceling it out or how long I had to do something. I had slipped out of time, and felt strangely refreshed because of it.

# Ripples on the River*

One morning of this steamy summer I was standing on the swimming dock on the edge of the river that runs along the back edge of our property. It was early, but the sun was, even then, pounding bright heat into my face. My cat MaChree was, as usual, quietly eating grass, and it was the only sound I could hear in the thick stillness. Standing thus, still and empty of thought, I noticed the ripples in the river at my feet.

At that part of the river the current is definite and vigorous, its haste visible with leaves and white patches of pine foam speedily rushing to the lake. It can be mesmerizing simply to watch this parade rushing past. But – just a few feet from the dock stairs where we descend to swim - I noticed the ripples, spiral upon spiral, marking where an eddy turns inward from the current and travels back up the river, paralleling the rushing current going down. In fact, when swimming, we often ride the eddy upwards, then plunge out into the current to be carried down quickly, looking for the spot to turn into the eddy again so as not to be carried too far down the river. Over and over, we make a circling game of it in the clean refreshing current.

As I watched it that morning, however, I thought of something else. When the spiral ripples leave the fast current and dance inwards, turning back up the river almost as swiftly as the current going down, I thought of how similarly life is lived, almost (or often) without knowing it. I thought of how we are all rushing along in the one fast current, passing some, dropping back with others, and then – at some point – sliding over to the edge of it. Then we find ourselves swirling off into a completely different, even opposite direction from where we thought we were going. One unexpected obstacle, one surprise attraction, one compelling idea – and suddenly we are floating at a different pace and in a different direction.

There is a strange and lovely beauty in all this – not a predictable beauty, or anything we might call "beautiful" in our common understanding of that word – but beauty there is nonetheless. In its unknown power and preference, the swirling ripples in our small river announce how Life is living us and not the opposite, not how we usually think of ourselves "living life". No – the ripples in the river remind me that Life lives us with beauty and pain, with love and the loss of love, and with the poignant glory at the dashing of our small insistencies. Floating with the eddy, rushing with the current, it is all one movement. It is all one Life.

*dedicated to Irene Thomas, who passed over into the next life hours before this was written.*

# No Endings

Standing in the silent lovely grounds of SoulWinds on one of the cooling evenings we have been having a bit too early, I began to notice the endings of all that I'd appreciated so much during the summer. The bee balm, the pink mallow, the luxurious fullness of trees, the butterflies and hummingbirds – for weeks they had filled my eyes with a particular joy, and on this evening I saw the fading, just as it began.

The end of summer is full of a peculiar sadness, just as the end of winter holds a definite joy. Yet – we go through this, year after year after year – and it's as if we somehow forget the cycle when each experience arises. Standing there, I had the thought "nothing ever ends," and remembered the theme of Mordecai Richler's story of Duddy Kravitz: "death ends a life, but not a relationship." This would be true of our relationship with the earth, with her cycles, on which our living depends.

But I had another, more poignant lesson in "no endings" a few weeks ago. On the early morning walk down Old Mill Rd., our dog Kai raced off toward something in the grass, not an unusual occurrence. By the time we caught up to her, a young wounded rabbit was trying desperately to hop away from her, with little success. Joan quickly took Kai away, and I pursued the rabbit, who was crying in pain when I reached her. Slowly I wrapped her in my jacket, and laid her on my beating heart, holding her wounded leg very tenderly. We thought that she might have been hit by a car. Almost as soon as I snuggled her on my chest, she settled peacefully, her ears and head just emerging from the jacket-wrap, her feet securely in my hands, her eyes searching my face. I was a kilometer from home. I walked slowly, trying not to jolt her. I will never forget the feeling of tender vulnerability she gave to me on that walk – the utter privilege of holding her and giving her safety, the certainty of some deep visceral connection that I am only just learning to experience with animals, all animals. They are the primal wise ones, and I have everything to learn from them.

Reaching home, Joan prepared the cat carrier with hay, lettuce, carrots and water while I held her. We placed her as gently as we could on the hay, and then in a shady place outside. We checked her every hour that day; twice she turned herself, and tried the lettuce. But by five o'clock, she was gone. She stretched out in perfect rabbit form, and gave in to the internal injuries we suspected, but we could not determine their extent, and wanted to give her a chance.

We were bereft, as if she'd lived with us a long time. We took her in our arms and thanked her. We took awhile to determine what we should do with her. Then I remembered the young fisher I'd encountered several times in a bend of the river where I go for utter solitude and to write. She was part of the cycle; so was he. In the early dark, we took her, still warm, and laid her on a rock close to where I encounter him. In the morning, she was gone – back into the life cycle of which we are all a part.

There are no endings.

# Nature's Pacing

When there weren't so many ways to bypass it, winter was the time for slowing down our human systems as well as the natural ones. Activities became confined to home and work. Evenings were slow and dark, with sleep beginning early and lasting long. Snow, as we still recognize today if we spend any time in it at all, creates its own deep silence, which refreshes mind and soul.

Like every success story, our technological achievements carry a shadow as well as a gift. Instead of the greater leisure originally promised by the invention of "helpful" gadgets, our "gadgets" require more attention and care than anyone ever imagined. They often seem to own us rather than the other way around. The general and most common cry of our way of life is "I don't have time." Our days have lost rhythms and structures, simple ones such as meals together, rest or reading times, storytelling or singing after supper. The loss of common rhythms fragments not only relationships, but causes individuals to live in a state of almost constant inner conflict, pulled in many directions at once, eventually leading to illness of one kind or another.

Recent scientific research bears this out. It has been found that human beings run on what are called "ultradian rhythms." In simplest terms it means that – even throughout a single day – we need a rhythm of effort and recovery, effort and recovery, in order to be in tune with what is best for our health, mental and physical. The period of time that is best for efforting is about ninety minutes; then a break of some kind allows us to return with energy to what needs doing. Even our sleep moves in shifting waves without our being aware of it.

But the constant moving, going, doing of our present day, enhanced by pressures and opportunities offered by technology and a swirl of opportunity, seduce us into thinking we can ignore the way we are biologically made. And we can – for awhile. But the fundamental pulse of life – of everything that lives in this universe – has its claim on us human beings, whether we choose to move with it or not. Rhythmicity is, after all, our inheritance.

I stand outside among the majestic trees that now seem rooted in snow. At night, when snow shines with its particular silent light, I feel their stillness moving into me, filling my veins with rest beyond what I can achieve in the busyness of my days. I know that the trees have drawn all their sap, their lifeblood, down into their roots until the spring sun calls it up again, and I look for ways to do the same. In this way I resonate with nature's pacing, even for a few moments.

# Living the River

Whenever someone asks me about where I live, I say – first off – "I live on a river." A look of awe with a sound of "ah" emerges on the face and from the mouth of my visitor. When people come for the first time, we often show them through the house, and there is always the moment when they see the river for the first time, see how close it is, how present from every room on that end of the house. Invariably they stop and stand, looking as if worlds of meaning and association are flooding their eyes.

Living on a river's edge has been an experience of fresh learning for me. When we were first looking for property, it was a lake we sought. Now I am wrapped in the river's flow of seasons, and wouldn't consider a lake at all, with its exposure, and its noisy toys. The river is a living presence and attracts its own kind. We commonly see beavers, otters, mink and fox. Bears regularly swim across, in one direction or another, uninterested in our small lives. Four different species of ducks mate and give birth there every spring. Loons and Geese return, nesting on the river's edge, dangerously visible. Great Blue Herons glide up and down, or stand still fishing, hiding in plain sight. Hawks, Crow, Ravens, Wild Turkeys and recently Eagles soar and swoop for our eager binoculars. Songbirds too numerous to name weave music like a garment, wrapping morning and evening.

Through all of this, we sit at the edge, knowing our place as witnesses only, or we swim in summer. The river flows, slowly or swiftly, clean and cool, especially on the hottest days. Dragon and Damsel flies adore its surface with their pretty winged dances. There is only the sound of water; no engines can despoil the purity of this part of the river because of the bridge below, the rapids above where we are. Fish are visible; frogs and turtles testify to the river's health.

This river is a teacher and a healer. Sitting in the swinging chair hour after hour, allowing the quiet to still my frenzied mind and calm my rushing body, I notice first of all that the river flows one way only, constant, faithful. "There is no going back," she whispers. The river is Life; the river is Time. The river carries and comforts, and – when that moment comes – flows on into the lake without resistance, without holding back a drop of herself.

Living the River is all this and more. I notice again and again how opposite it is with me. I want to hold back my own flow, cling to time and schedule, force things to happen outside their own natural flow. I want time to slow down, sometimes even to stop. Daily, the river tells me otherwise. It brings me back from pointless resistance. Living the River is the gift of flow and surrender, among teeming and irrefutable life. This is what goes on.

# Gauging the Day

Every morning without fail my cat MaChree meows loudly and persistently to go out. When I come to open the door, he will most often stand there, sniffing the air (often for minutes) before slowly placing one paw on the doorsill, a deliberate, seemingly meditative move towards the place he really wants to go.

Most mornings it is difficult for me to be patient with this daily confronting of the morning. I stand over him, holding the door open, saying more loudly than is necessary "MaChree! Go Out!" No effect. He is lost in some sniffing contemplation. Other times, I have been known to tap his behind with the sole of my foot, gently pushing him out so the door can close. Even then, he will often sit still just outside the door, staring and – it seems – tasting the air.

Lately I've found myself having a different thought about MaChree's way of beginning the outdoor element of his day. When I get up, I move automatically into the day's movements: rebuilding the fire; filling the kettle, getting the animals' breakfasts, re-filling the dry humidifier after the night. Among these necessary tasks, I might or might not notice the beauty of the early light, or the way the night's snow has outlined the trees, or the thermometer announcement in the morning dark. But – unlike MaChree – I haven't been stopping to gauge the day. I haven't stopped to breathe before I begin my activity, nor have I stood to allow the morning stillness to enter my being like fuel for what the day might bring. In other words, I haven't tasted the air around me, seeing what's afoot for this day.

I am wondering now how the day might be different if I imitated MaChree's slow start. What would change, if – between waking and plunging into motion – I stopped and noticed the world, outside and inside.

The increasing speed that takes over our days, taking us riding as if on a swollen and uncontrollable river, is mentioned frequently now in journalism and in company. Perhaps it's an insight that comes with age...but not when people younger by decades also encounter the problem of not enough time. If the pace of our day isn't serving us, then what are we serving by allowing ourselves to be swept up and along by demands over which there seems little control?

MaChree refuses to leave his reflective space, even with a push from behind. He won't be hurried through his contemplation of the world. I, on the other hand, can be diverted from my purpose by a ringing telephone, mind instantly jumping in with questions and wondering. And there's the difference. There is a place where mind has no place, and it's there that I aspire to go. What MaChree enjoys by nature, I must learn by steady and faithful practice. And I begin by learning to gauge the day in early light – or dark.

# Every Day the Same Walk

I suppose there aren't more than four or five mornings of the year that we don't walk from our house on CloverLeaf Road down Old Mill Road to Elvin Johnson Park on the northern edge of Halls Lake. Those are the mornings when the temperature drops, usually January or early February, below -18. When it's as cold as that, breathing is difficult and not worth risking. On some days we wait until the temperature rises to that; it might be noon. But always we walk the same road, though in spring our faces are masked with mosquito netting. All the rest of the year, it is a walk of early morning, greeting all the varieties of weather. Two years ago, in August, the road was littered with trees and debris from the tornado, and we had to climb over huge dying trees to reach the houses on the lake's edge to see if anyone was hurt.

Some friends from the city own a cottage on the other side of the river, and they come up pretty often for weekends and longer periods in summer. At the beginning, they wanted to walk with us in the mornings, but soon they suggested we walk the other way, or take yet a third route – they were out for variety. These communal walks quickly came to an end – we wanted the sameness of the morning route. Other people stare at us, too polite to comment when we tell them this, but we are now into our sixth year of walking the same route without fail every morning.

Others' questions, as is so often the case, cause me to think seriously about why the same walk every day. The first response is that it is never the same walk. There is always something new on this one patch of road. Some days we have Arctic hare dashing back and forth across the road as if to tease us into following; then they disappear for days. We hear the Merlin falcon screeching most mornings, and we've rescued turtles in danger of being crushed by cars. The colors, shapes and patterns of growth and grass change every day, every season. A few times, we've slapped our sides and shouted at bears to get off the road and they do. We watch the seasons turning; lilies, trillium, milkweed in their dramatic seasons. When we reach the park the lake is always, always different. Geese and gulls, ducks and loons greet or run away from us. We stand and breathe, or give the dog Kai a good run, reveling in the ecstatic movement of her joy in running. But there are other reasons.

We live in a world of novelty, of throwing out things because we tire of them when they're still perfectly useful. We are surface people, bored by repetition and unable to settle in quiet. We want breadth, not depth. We fear silence and fill it as soon as possible. We multi-task, we cannot stop, we are sooooo busy. So doing the same walk every day is foreign for many – isn't there more to see? What if the "more to see" is right there, before our eyes, walking the same walk every day?

And really, isn't life itself, getting up in the morning, going to bed at night, at its heart walking the same road every day? What else is there?

# Embering

There used to be an ancient Christian practice called "Ember Days." These days occurred at the changing of the seasons; around the equinoxes and the solstices. They also flourished at a time when life found its rhythms around nature, not around shopping holidays. When electricity and information technology took us all over, that cyclic, predictable rhythm was lost to many of us in the developed world, though it still exists in places less developed than ours. We could do as much at night as in daylight; we could do as much in winter as in summer. Productivity, disposable money, speed – these became the standard of "the good life."

But this "good life" also has its shadow side. As the outer life speeds up, inner life is lost. Silence, solitude and pondering anything for longer than a minute is considered a waste of time. Constant socializing – the mindless chatter of "drinks" and parties – is the standard of what passes for communication. Anyone seeking quiet is suspect. Grief and tears are also suspect, "getting on with it" the only things to do.

In the face of such superficial engagement, I have been finding myself pulled back to the "Ember Days" of my early life. The point of what I now call "embering" is simply this: to draw back from the socializing and from as many external demands as one can (emails a big one for me) and to increase quiet. Going for a walk alone, standing in the woods, turning off all external sound while in your own house, spending more time in reading what turns you towards your inner self, meditating – these would be possible Ember Day activities. As would being aware of your actions rather than moving through the day automatically, resting, and allowing the answering machine to take messages. The fact that it's so difficult for us to imagine some of these practices is itself an indication of how enslaved we've become, how cut off from inner wisdom. Ember days, as the name implies, are meant to open a space where we can encounter our own inner fire, the spark of our own spirit-flame. These are meant to be days of recovery and refiring.

Recently I put my words into practice, I moved for twenty-four hours to the tiny trailer that sits on the edge of our property. First of all I slept for twelve hours, wrapped in the deepest silence – an indication in itself of how badly I needed an ember day. The rest of the time was spent tracking what had become of my hassled and over-worked spirit. I did this by writing and by being present to what was happening just in this moment, using some of the ways named above.

Yes, I could definitely see my tactics of avoidance and resistance. The impulse to return phone calls and emails once I felt rested was strong. But I stayed….and stayed…and at the end caught a glimpse of that glowing ember that had gotten lost in the outer fray. Perhaps it's time to look again at the outer wisdom that offers peace and wholeness.

# Common Milkweed

As I walk each day along the almost traffic-free Old Mill Road leading to Halls Lake, I notice the subtle signs of the seasons turning. Where once the evening primrose, purple vetch and field daisy were my sidelong companions, proclaiming the abundance of summer, now the joe pye-weed, purple aster, and common milkweed are in their less noticeable full bloom. Monarch butterflies are in feasting time.

But it is the common milkweed that grabs and holds my attention. Lime green pods, shapely and textured, grow more full every day, grow toward bursting point. From other years I know that these pods house thousands and thousands of downy seeds, pure white, tightly packed and silky to the touch. The tiny brown seed itself is carried on the breeze to a new growing place by those feathery wings of down, catching the wind upon release from the pod.

The poet, Mary Oliver, compares milkweed to "a country of dry women," evoking the image of growing into a fullness of life so abundant that we too reach a bursting point of having received so much that we can do nothing more but give back to the world, scattering our seeds to the wind without the need to know where they'll land or how they'll fare in growing. This is, indeed, the natural order of everything, a pulse like breathing, this receiving and giving back, receiving and giving back.

But contemplating the fruitfulness of this supposedly common weed raises a question for me too: what seeds am I scattering? Sometimes, when – in Newfoundland parlance - I am having a "crooked" moment or even day – here in Ontario this is called "cranky"- I can very easily sow the toxic seeds of discontent, complaining, blaming, criticism, and continual fault-finding. Most days, I am inclined to scatter seeds of affirmation, appreciation, joy in having enough, peace in my own soul, awe at the land around me. For while the milkweed has no choice about the nature of her seeds, I do, and that's what it means to be human.

There is nothing common about the common milkweed. It is rich in its presence and in its legacy, food for the most royal of butterflies, the monarch. If you are lucky enough to see the moment when a dry milkweed pod slowly opens, releasing seed after seed to the wind - which could take half a day or more – you will be astounded at the delicate power of something as common as the milkweed. May your heart be moved.

# Bread and Labyrinths

Anyone who ventures to read this piece with so mysterious a title is adventurous indeed. Yet, in what I am writing about here, these two are reflections of one another, as you'll see if you persevere.

When I was a growing girl, my mother would rise at 4 am every Saturday morning to make the week's bread. In those pre-dawn hours, dark and silent, with everyone in the household asleep and will little danger of drafts or small, poking fingers, she began the liturgy of transformation that is perhaps the most ancient in history: the delicate attention, though-by-thought, to yeast and sugar, flour, salt and water, that becomes the miracle of nourishment for family. By the time the rest of us rose, around 8 am on a Saturday (this was sleeping in then) we sat before plates of fresh, steaming bead with butter and molasses, enough to sustain us for the day. Sometimes – since I grew up in Newfoundland – we were given the special treat of toutens: pancake-sized bread dough fried to a crispy brown on both sides, with the same delicious additions.

Only now, as an adult, watching a friend mindfully step through the magical process of making bread, have I come to a deeper awareness of the significance of bread itself, and how the making of it nurtures both body and soul. The instant expectation of everything in our culture makes bread-making a counter-cultural, even subversive activity. "No," we are saying," no – I will not succumb to the instant, chemically preserved, mindless loaf of soggy dough." Making bread from scratch slows time, deepens awareness, gives time for love and care to become part of the mixture, the kind of energy needed more than ever in our speedy, over-filled days.

In these and other ways, bread-making is very similar to walking a labyrinth. We start at a defined place with a clear intention. The framework, the ingredients, are present. After that, it's all attention and dedication. Distraction loses you the connection with the present moment that ensures a satisfying outcome. Walking a labyrinth, you come to corners and turns that require your attention to make. Inattention risks wrong turns and confusing blocks to your journey. Making bread, the same is true, with the painful possible outcome of a fallen loaf, or a dense, unbaked lump emerging from the oven. Both bread and labyrinths are about centre: staying centered, moving to and out of the centre, dwelling in the centre for a few satisfying moments.

Watching the bread-making process taking place over a whole morning, with waiting and checking, and spraying and rising, making its delicate way towards warm nourishment, I find a particular easiness of atmosphere. We are joyous, spontaneous, unpressured, looser in expectation, jocular and tender. This bread, I think today, is a material manifestation of soul transformed.

# Animal Gifts

One of the best parts of living in this county is the amount of wildlife that we are privileged to encounter almost every day. While some people, out of fear, don't see this as an advantage at all, many (I am one) who recognize the particular grace of wild presences revel in the vibrancy of living so close to nature. They were – as the common wisdom goes – here first, after all. And as we come more and more to understand the intricate weaving necessary to the future of planet earth, our eyes open to the mystery of how we depend on one another. All our futures are tied in with one another's; animal, plant, human.

So it enriches the everyday life of routine work and household tasks when we are given the opportunity – and see it as gift – to be in the presence of a wild animal or bird. Over our years of being here, many such encounters send us into a questioning of what gifts these animals are offering us, offering the world. Since this question has already been asked by indigenous peoples everywhere and for many centuries, we ask it too, and consult the accumulated wisdom of response to which we now have access. One such collection of wisdom is the Medicine Cards, (Bear and Company, 1988), a worn-out book never far from our kitchen bookshelf.

In late fall we met six wild turkeys on Little Hawk Lake Rd. and had to stop the car for them. This was unusual enough to send us to the book, and we discovered that Turkey is associated with the practice of "give-away," since every part of a turkey is used to give life. Talking about it, we realized that there was much we needed to give away as well, and meeting these wild turkeys influenced our Christmas practices. The appearance of a grouse is an invitation to enter fully into life, seeing it as a dance, spiraling us through time and space, something we can either move with or resist. The large number of rabbits and hares we are meeting this season caused us to look up their message, which is to face your fears and to stop running from them. Deer – and we have come face-to-face with many – remind us to find a gentleness of spirit and to stop pushing so hard to get others to change; accept them as they are. What a useful reminder! Bears – and we are awed by their number and closeness this spring, watching them come close enough to sniff the back door – are large messengers of the power of introspection. They tell us that the inner cave of your soul is where all answers lie, in that feminine cave of receptivity. Entering the silence you find out how to make your goals concrete realities.

There are many ways we can respond to the presence of such a variety of animals and birds close to our living spaces and ourselves. Seeing them as messengers and receiving their message is one way that we can experience our own physical and spiritual connection with all living things. We come to know that we are really all in this together, and the loss of even one species diminishes our world and ourselves. But seeing animals and birds more closely, valuing their presences, enriches our human lives beyond what we know.

# Night-Gift in Day Light

When I was abruptly awakened by my housemate early on a Saturday morning, I knew it had to be something out of the ordinary, so I swung out of bed immediately and ran to the sun room – three walls of glass overlooking a circle of red pines and the other trees surrounding our home. Whispering behind me, she said "don't move – look at the bird feeder."

But the bird feeder was empty, and as our eyes surveyed the land surrounding the house, I saw it, a bulky brown bird walking awkwardly over the snow under more of the pines. Then he swooped – silent and large as only owls can be in their flight – right to the bird feeder only three or four feet from the window where we watched. Still as night, he found our eyes through the glass and gazed into them for what seemed a long time. We hardly breathed and couldn't speak. We were in the presence of the Great Gray Owl – later confirmed in our bird book and again through a birder friend.

In full daylight, we felt the impact of this imposing night-presence. By habit we each were observing and trying to remember his shape, his eyes, his various stripes and colors, but it was the still, opaque, blackness of his pupils, ringed with yellow, fixing on us with purpose that made this moment an encounter. Afterwards, we both revealed that in those moments when we could not take our eyes away from his, we each felt a timelessness, a sense that this moment gave us a unique connection with true wildness, serene and steadying.

And also raw. Later that day while we played with our small black cat in the white snow, he led us to feathers in the same spot where we'd seen the Great Gray Owl on the snow's surface. They were tiny gray-blue downy feathers, and we realized that the owl had taken a chickadee in that spot just before coming to sit on our feeder, where we'd encountered him.

Many times that day we spoke about the uniqueness of this visitation, searching for the significance of such a visit. In Native and other spiritual traditions, owls are associated with intuition and wisdom for their ability to be so silent and to see in the dark. Because of the unusual acuity of these skills, owls know what many other animals don't know, and their clear seeing and hearing is remarkable even in the animal world. Sharply aware and hunting at night, it is unusual to see them in daylight. For all these reasons, this Great Gray Owl turned our attention to our own lives in a remarkable way, making us think of how we might be using similar skills without knowing it.

With both of us engaged in the helping professions, we realized that we too sense many things about the lives of others before they know it themselves and that we must often be silent about those things. We too help people dig into their own darkness, waiting with them until light arrives. All of this the Great Gray Owl brought before us on an ordinary Saturday when we were expecting just the usual winter activities of a day off. In the day's light, we received a night gift. And a reminder that nature's offerings, unlike our own, come suddenly and without plan, and that recognizing them in their moment, for who they are, enriches our lives without measure.

# Abundance and the Landfill

We have been notified that our landfill will close in April. Whenever I go there now, I am even more aware of the piles – small hills and hills – of waste and excess and cast-aside things that have seen their day, at least according to someone's standard. Sometimes I wonder what all this will do to the soil as it slowly disintegrates and who will find it all in centuries to come and what will it tell them of us?

Sober thoughts for Christmas, though it's after Christmas now, and we have had our abundance. This year, along with material abundance, which we attempt to lessen every year and yet it still seems abundant, we chose and enjoyed abundance of time. We did not rush to visit, nor to have visitors; we were leisurely in mornings and evenings, and slept longer. Most days of the season we were able to snowshoe or ski for a couple of hours. The beauty of how the snow stayed on the trees as we went through silent woods not only wasn't boring; it was positively nourishing, a restful break from noise while bodies were moving with healthy vigor. Without work commitments, time slowed down and we were slow to fill it up.

The word "abundance" seemed to occur often in our conversations over the past month. I read somewhere during this time that the earth at this moment has the capacity to feed all people and animals who live on the planet, if those of us who have more than others would agree to have less. Though I have heard this often before, I was particularly stirred by it this season as I heard more and more people complain about having too much food, too many presents to give and even receive, and that much of what they received they didn't really want. The escalating phenomenon of Boxing Week sales tips this materialistic culture just over the edge of acceptable.

There are abundances that we need more than the kind that overflows the landfill. (This word always makes me want to ask why the land needs to be filled – but it's not the land's need – it's ours.) We need an abundance of slow time, an abundance of rest and the nurturing silence of nature. We need an abundance of peace in our relationships and respect for the differences that divide us and don't need to. We need an abundance of creative expression, the kind that satisfies the soul beyond anything material possessions can ever do. We need healthy food and the occasional feast, not a continual one. These abundances won't be filling the landfills until they have to be closed.

This year, when I asked a friend of mine what she was giving people for Christmas, she surprised me by saying that she was giving time. She was offering her full attentive presence to people she loved but never had enough time with. Another friend gave trees, this year – certificates of planting in the friend's name, trees that could actually be visited and that gave to the earth as well as the person. A third gave time by making something that the person needed, like a walking stick.

The overflowing landfills surrounding us formulate a question, at least for me: how can we de-escalate our material use of the earth and yet enjoy an abundance that has longer lasting effects than clothes, electronics, furniture or toys?

# The Price of Wonder

Spring is a contradictory season in the Alquonquin Highlands.

First there is the end of winter, the relief of it, the incredulity that takes over, when – suddenly one morning - the last vestige of snow has disappeared. April usually offers a few days of over-warmth, just to tease, when everything green leaps out of the ground, before frost returns for a few nights into May and June. But spring isn't held back by a few frosty nights, demonstrating the invincible gusto of growing things after winter's death-dealing cold. Buds, blossoms, catkins, fiddlehead ferns quickly stand forth into annunciation.

All of this would seem like paradise were it not for the presence of black flies and mosquitoes. If there is significant rain and humidity, as has been the case this year, they swarm in clouds around people and animals, hindering outdoor activities of almost any kind. Even hanging laundry outside becomes occasion for netting and spraying exposed body parts. This year, radio announcers in southern Ontario are warning cottagers of the number of black flies and mosquitoes waiting to greet them when they arrive, signaling how much more drastic are their numbers this year.

There is something perverse in this presence of buzzing pests in the midst of an otherwise paradise, but it is no more perverse than the nature of life itself. Much as we – in our quest for comfort and security and control of the environment for our own convenience – develop sprays and gadgets to control what we hope to eliminate, nature continues to evade our meager attempts. For in the face of Nature, in the face of this planet's intricate and delicate balancing acts, humans are still puny and short-sighted.

Anyone would say that black flies and mosquitoes are puny and short-sighted. But look how they challenge us, year after year after year affecting the shape and duration of our outdoor activities in arguably the most beautiful, the most uplifting season of spring.

And isn't this how life is, our daily renewal of hope and promise interrupted by the unforeseen prickles and bites of interruption and surprise? Black flies and mosquitoes, for all their irritating welts and itchy skin bumps and annoying buzzing are really just witnesses to the nature of life itself.

As I drive down winding and hilly Braeloch Road, ebullient and lush and almost blinding green like so many of the lesser-driven country roads, trees almost form a tunnel over the road and I am full of wonder and gratitude that I live in this place, of all the possible places on earth.

And then I slap at the mosquito that just bit my forehead at the hairline, and see my own blood smeared across my fingers. Ah, the price of wonder.

# Just Walking

One of the great delights of living in Haliburton County is the number of quiet country roads on which we can walk freely, surrounded mainly by forest, marsh and lakes, with only the occasional cottage. Traffic – especially on weekdays – is minimal and the only sound is birdsong. Having lived in cities for most of my life, I still find myself awed at the quiet that settles over me while walking these roads. Still, even here, I had something to learn before I could even recognize this particular gift.

I began by walking out of necessity, and found myself with a little edge of resentment that I "had" to walk – for health reasons. Exercise has always been a part of my life, but until I moved here, I belonged to a fitness club or gym of some kind. No need to now. Heating with wood provides plenty of "weight training", and kayaking several times a week – even in winter – makes for excellent upper body strength training. But cardio-vascular conditioning is enhanced in only one way if you're not a runner: engaging the whole body by walking.

I would have loved walking except that I was too busy. Work and plans, phone calls, ideas, tasks to be done around the house, emails to return, teaching online to be attended to. Where would I find a half hour to just walk? (Writing it now reminds me of what a momentum of activity was building and building, and how pathetic is the question "where would I find a half hour to 'just walk'?") But walk it had to be, so I began by walking with a tape player and listening to music or talks while I walked. Somehow, a nagging voice convinced me that this was less than helpful; that just walking had a benefit I was missing though

I didn't know what that could be. Next I decided to do without the headset and just take a tiny digital recorder so that I could record the brilliant ideas as they arose. And arise they did: many excellent ideas for work began to present themselves during the walks and for awhile I thought I'd found the balance. Between ideas I began to notice the landscape. I began to hear the melodies of birds. I began to notice the daily changes in the river along which I walked.

Then I became slowly aware that ideas while walking were dropping away, at least in the urgent necessity of recording them. My inner busyness began to settle almost as soon as I began to walk, and a calming joy took the place of urgency and haste. I receive this gift now almost every day, this gift of "just walking." Even when I walk the same quiet road for weeks on end, I see that the road is different every day. Plants emerge; trees change, water levels rise and fall; smells fill the air and then disappear, the birdsongs vary. Without knowing at all why, or needing to know, I return more refreshed than I did when I had a tape full of ideas.

And - oh yes – I now walk for an hour each day. A half hour is just too little.

# Winds of Life

People have been asking me about the name "SoulWinds" and why we have named our property by that name.

Several years ago I rented a small house near Huntsville, also in a forested area. On the property was a small pond which I frequented every day, usually about four o'clock in the afternoon, after a long day of solitary work. I would go to the pond and sit or stand, without moving, sometimes for nearly an hour as I transitioned out of concentrated writing back into the world of conversation and necessary household tasks. One evening I was standing there among the trees, wrapped in the sight of three beavers trying busily to build a dam at the point where the pond emptied into a small river, and I didn't notice how quickly the sky had changed. Rain began, and my first impulse was to race for the house. But it was a warm rain, so I decided to stay. A small spark of adventure kindled inside: who had decreed the need for shelter from rain anyway? I watched how the hard raindrops made dents in the water's surface as if it were a sheet of metal, even as they soaked me thoroughly in a matter of seconds. Then the sky changed again, turned a sickly shade of green, and the rain turned to hail, making pearls of the water this time. Wind whipped briefly around, twisting the very air, it seemed. Again I resisted the impulse to run back to the house.

Within five minutes both rain and hail ended, and the sun appeared, shocking in its brightness. The water was smooth as a mirror. Stillness characterized the whole landscape, as if the previous fifteen minutes hadn't happened at all. It was at this point that I named this small pond as "SoulWeather Pond." With a jolt of recognition I saw how similar the inner being, the soul, is subject to quickly changing vagaries of wind and weather, just as this small pond is subject to sudden and dramatic changes in outer weather. From that day on, I referred to that pond as "SoulWeather Pond", though I have not lived now for many years.

So it was no surprise that when we moved to Haliburton County two years ago, one of the first things we began to talk about was a name for the property. Like my experience with the pond, no name we could think of seemed to suit the property itself. We went through all the varieties of "Pine this and that", as well as "River-something" and "something Haven" – all good words but not for this patch of land on the Little Kennesis River. We gave up, and decided to wait until the land itself suggested a name of its own choosing.

A few weeks later we were sitting on the river bank late in the evening. The fire we'd built was burning down. Close to the ground was an evening stillness, but in the quiet of gaps in the conversation we began to hear the wind talking through the treetops. I remember we both looked up spontaneously. It had been a difficult move: many things had gone wrong and were continuing to do so; we had left behind many friends and knew no one here; we were both more tired than usual with one of us breaking her foot on moving day itself. Worn down, we listened – and heard the winds of life buffeting and nudging us forward. That's when the name "SoulWinds" came to us, and we immediately recognized it as fitting both our experience and the place.

# Words in the Woods

Lately I've been thinking about how nature is really the equivalent of what we normally think of as a book. When we go into nature with no agenda except to learn from it, to see what it contains, it's as if we open a book, and with that gesture open ourselves to whatever it has to say. When we read a book quickly, minds racing through words, very little of the message gets through. The same is true for being in a forest, or by a river or lake, or climbing a mountain: if our minds are somewhere else, the "writing" is really closed to us in any real and immediate way.

There are words in the woods. Not the way we usually think about a word; i.e., as a combination of letters communicating a recognizable layer of meaning, but a word of presence, of unmistakable being, of mutual recognition. Noticing any created thing – a tree, a blade of grass, an ant, a fox, a woodpecker – expands my own being in this world. Since I've begun to think about this, I've come across many writers, ancient and new, who experience the same "communion" in nature as we do when we read a book that pulls us in with interest and meaning.

But for many people, life is just too hectic, too rushed, too filled, to read the book of nature. I wonder what would happen if some of us who like to ponder and write our thoughts were to put actual letter-words in the woods inviting people to think differently about where they are and what's happening in that moment. For despite the busyness and the frantic pace, thousands of people come to forests, lakes and rivers every year, sensing – if unconsciously – their need for the natural world. We could make bridges with our words for those who don't have time for anything else. What if, for example, you were hiking on a quiet trail thinking about something else, when you noticed at the side of the path the words "I am so glad you're here" spelled out in tiny logs or "stop and warm your heart" or "stand and look around?"

Still, there's something to be said as well for the atmosphere of a natural setting if you really need to think, if you're pre-occupied or solving a necessary problem. Even without directly knowing about it, the silence of nature – emphasized and enriched by bird calls or the sound of running water or crashing waves – offers a spaciousness for thought to settle, for questions to arise and even sometimes be answered. The silence of trees and all other expressions of the natural world open wide spaces in us, and the possibilities are infinite.

# Languages of the World

It used to be that people who spoke other "foreign" languages were considered sophisticated, educated or somehow larger than those who spoke only the language they were born into. Speaking another language was seen to expand a sense of all that was possible in the world. But standing still in the woods has revealed to me something that has become even more important than learning French or Italian or Spanish, however cosmopolitan that might seem. Standing still in the woods has taught me that there are languages that leap out at me, begging to be learned, just around the small property that is SoulWinds, where I live.

Now it feels compelling to learn oak and pine and hemlock, cedar and fir- all of which are colloquialisms for the language of Tree. Then there is Bear and Fox, Wolf and Fisher and Mink, Otter and Weasel - all quite different in their languages and in their distinctions of communication. Lately I am listening to Woodpecker language, as well as Purple Finch, Pine Grosbeak, Blue Jay, White-Throated Sparrow and Raven and Crow and Turkey Vulture – the bird languages that give me both companionship and warning. This summer I had quite a serious conversation with Cardinal Flowers about their protected status, and with Common Milkweed and Bluebell and Bloodroot – by now you are catching my drift. And though I never thought this would happen, I am learning to converse with Dragon and Damsel Flies, Carpenter Ants, Giant SwallowTail and Mourning Cloak butterflies, and even Mosquitoes and Clusterflies. Suddenly I realize that the river and the soil I walk on are aware of me, and trying to reveal secrets to me every day when I'm not too thought-bound to hear them. I am well-along in River languages and have spoken snake for years now. Darkness – with no artificial light whatsoever – is also a compelling conversationalist.

What would our world be like, I wonder, if we included every created thing in our human conversations? If we had Entire Earth Immersion schools, (including Sky and Stars and Planets), not just French Immersion classes? Out of all the questions we encounter in the run of a day, this one seems as important as any.

Before the ground swallows me again, I want to learn as many languages of hers as I can. I want to run towards that homecoming as to a banquet for which I've managed to find the proper clothes, or to a destination I bought a ticket to a long time ago, and am now more than ready to undertake the journey.

The languages of the world sound the most splendid symphony we humans can comprehend hearing. Not Babel, but profound Beauty. I intend to be more than multi-lingual as I approach elder age; I intend to be fluent and comfortable in as many languages I have time to learn.

# The River Leaf

The river leaf began her life not knowing the river at all.

She burst forth one day, the tiniest of red buds on a giant old tree known as red maple. She could see other tiny buds around her, knew she wasn't alone, and felt the hard brown branch on which they all saw each other for the first time. It was a big branch, thick and long, and it stretched out over something they couldn't quite see. Yet, from the beginning, they were surrounded by the river's voice without knowing what it was.

The tiny maple bud pushed up and out. She unfurled, and spread. She inhabited the air around her like a fan. Sometimes she stood still, seeing the multitude of other leaves filling out this old tree in garments of glory. Some of them were close to her, touching her, and she felt glad. Sometimes a slow breeze moved them all together and apart, together and apart, and they knew themselves to be dancing. And sometimes a loud wind thrashed them together without mercy, and they could only bend and blow with it until that wind blew itself out and left for other trees. Rain was welcomed for its softening, its cleansing, and its nourishment.

And always the river sang, just below their knowing.

Days and weeks went by in the rhythm of wind and light, rain and dark. The maple leaf grew large, with a stem powerful enough to stand up to the wind, to taste the rain, and to laugh at the strong breezes that sometimes arrived suddenly with no warning at all.

And all the time the river was singing, going only one way, unnoticed by the leaf and her companions on that one strong and hardy branch.

Then one day the maple leaf felt a new feeling. It was the cold. It began slowly at first, but then – everything was filled with it – the wind, the rain – even her stem where she was attached to her branch. The cold made her feel shaky, and then – and then – she noticed that her color was changing. She could hardly recognize herself. Her green was going. Yellow – what was that? And now red was seeping in. Who was this red leaf? She was so taken up with her own changes that she forgot to look around her, and when she did, she was shocked to find that all her companions were looking unfamiliar, different shades of different colors, like herself.

Finally she was all red, a shining, luminous red, but she still found it hard to think of herself that way. What could she do but say yes to this new color? But wait – something else was happening. Her stem – her proud strong attachment to the tree – was loosening. It was coming away. She felt unsteady. Everything familiar had disappeared when she wasn't looking, it seemed. The red maple leaf tried to huddle and cling to the only familiar thing left in her world – and she couldn't.

The coldest wind of all came. And the river still sang.

The red maple leaf floated for what seemed an endless time, and to her it was. She was lifted one night – not quite gently - from her old battered branch, and placed on the invisible wings of the wind. There was nothing to do but move with this unfamiliar current that she could neither see nor hold onto. But it moved her somewhere, and all she knew was that she was still alive. Nothing else was left. As she floated downward and downward, a new voice came into her hearing, the voice that had always been there, faint and distant. The red maple leaf seemed to hear this voice for the first time as she was laid on its moving sound. The river took her with a violent shiver.

Where once she had stood still, moving only to the wind's whim but always feeling secure in her solid connection to the branch, now the red maple leaf was swiftly swung into a fast moving current. Nothing held her but the water. Shapes she had never seen before passed into her knowing but she could no more choose to hold them or stay with them than she could get back to her branch. Who could know how big the world really is? she thought. And here I was thinking that my branch was the world, and that I would always be firmly attached to it.

The red maple leaf wasn't alone on the water, but her companions were now not the familiar shapes of maple leaves like herself, or the squirrels who had raced by her often enough to be considered part of her tree. Passing her in the swift flow were sticks of all sizes, leaves in shapes she'd never seen before, white foam that threatened to envelop her completely. Then there were the birds – ducks and herons and hawks and loons. Beneath her were the strangest shapes of all – creatures actually under the water, moving with it or against it: fish, beaver, otter, mink, snake. Some of them moved above and below at will, she saw. But the red maple leaf could not choose her path in the river. She could only move as the river moved her, and no amount of resistance could change this truth.

Gradually, the red maple leaf found that the river not only had a flow, but a rhythm of its own. Light and dark changed places again and again, just as they had when she was lodged in her tree. She could count on that. Then she noticed that the river had faces other than the fast flow. She was often pushed into eddies where she had little spaces of motionless and soundless slowing while the river swirled her around more softly and became quiet, almost like a lullaby. The red maple leaf treasured these times especially, though she knew they would not last – and she knew that she'd come to them again. She also became aware that whenever the river came to a corner, its voice became louder and its flow a little faster, as if making an effort to take the turn. And that when the turn was done, she could expect a slowing down, a restful, slowing movement when she could rest on the water.

Once she was mistaken for food by one of the underwater creatures and was pulled under before being rejected for that purpose. For awhile, she was fully immersed in water. No air. Strange shapes and sounds. After that immersion, the red maple leaf began to think of herself differently. Her world had changed so completely that she could no longer think of herself as a red maple leaf. She realized that she had become, instead, a river leaf.

The river leaf continued to flow with the river, each day surrendering to wherever it took her. She began to enjoy the sun on her surface, and even the cold breezes didn't seem as bad as when she was high up on her branch. Sometimes the river took her into crevices and corners, stuck in the debris that was floating along with her. She never knew how long she'd be there, but she knew that the river never stopped, and that she would move into its flow again. That fact, like dark and light, was to be trusted. And one more thing she realized was also to be trusted: the river flowed in only one direction. She would never see her branch, or her tree, again.

The river's voice became the river leaf's song. The river's adventures were her adventures. She knew herself now only as belonging to the river, not to the tree, that faint memory. One day, she noticed that the current was slowing and slowing, and she could no longer see the familiar scenes along the river's edges. She could only see a vast expanse of water, and it was no longer moving.

Gradually, the river leaf came to rest among the tall striped grasses where the river became the lake. She felt hidden there, safe – but not in the old way of being attached to the tree. The river leaf felt a fullness, a completion of something she couldn't quite name, but the grasses helped her to know it, and to hold it. No more wanting anything else but what she had, no more wanting to be anywhere else but where she was.

One more change awaited the little river leaf who'd lived the fullness of her days. Now even the red began to fade – the red that was once so strange and threatening – and then familiar. A crystal coating of white covered her one night, and just before morning she saw that she had been painted in the most delicate of lacy patterns, and beneath those patterns, she was no longer red, but gold. She was astounded at her own beauty, knowing that she had not made herself so, but that she had been made so. And that she was ready to begin again.

And the river sang her into ending, and later – into beginning.

The following essays have all been published previously as indicated

# Little Kennisis Run*

There is a magic river deep in the Alquonqin Highlands in Haliburton County. Flowing out of Big Hawk Lake at the end of a sideroad that parallels the river all the way, the Little Kennisis River, known locally as the Bubbling Hawk, rushes and dawdles – depending on the season and the MNR – into Halls Lake, one of the deepest fresh water lakes in Ontario.

At the beginning of the river, where it leaves Big Hawk Lake, is a historic log chute, one of only a very few left from the logging days of Ontario and Quebec. Logs were floated on Big Hawk Lake until they could be pushed into the chute, where they began their journey to Stouffer's Mill, about half way down the river's course. Three years ago, this battered chute was restored, and it now occupies the central place in a park built to showcase its history. Walking paths and picnic tables make the visit to this history compelling, as compelling as the booming sound that the river makes there as it leaves the lake. Cross the bridge over the chute, where you can look closely into its roaring spray, and you can begin a steep climb that turns into one of the most spectacular hiking trails of the county – the Crests of Kennisis, part of an interconnecting trail system of Haliburton County.. If you have all day, you can walk right to Stanhope on the North Shore Road, and many do. The views and the trail itself wrap you in beauty and in the life of the land at every step in every season.

The Little Kennisis River is famous for something else in this area. With both its bubbling rapids and its slow meandering, tubers of all ages, shapes and experience – not to speak of their tube conveyances

– make for the river almost every day of summer. It offers civilized choices: the rapids are bumpy but not dangerous, and if you still don't want to chance them, you can start below where they end and just give yourself up to the river's pace. An hour and twenty-minutes – faster on a high-river day – takes you right into Halls Lake. Truck-tire tubes, large, handled speedboat tubes, fancy plastic loungers with arm holes for your refreshment – they all float down the river. Refreshment can be anything from water, coffee and pop to beer trailing along on a string under the tube to keep it cool. People float down carrying their dogs and children, and once we saw in infant in arms.

Whole camps bring their guests to tube the Little Kennisis. Once we were lounging on our dock (and by now you know that we live on this river's bank) when we heard giggles and screams indicating a large group floating down towards us. Indeed, it was a group of thirty- five Koreans from a close-by camp, few of whom could speak English, and they were experiencing something unheard of in their culture. They were excited and scared, and as they came close to us, many of them floated into the significant eddy that adorns our corner. We spent a pleasant afternoon standing waist-deep in the water, swinging tubes back out into the current so that they could continue onto the bridge, where a camp employee was picking them up. No English needed!

But what is it that makes me call the river magic? Living here all year round, we are especially grateful that the Little Kennisis River is too shallow to accommodate motorized water conveyances. Canoes and kayaks (including our own) adorn the river in three seasons (and we have been known to kayak on Christmas Eve), but motorboats, jet skis, and – above all – pontoon boats find it impossible to explore very far up our river. Not that, every now and then, someone doesn't try to see how far they can come up the river from the lake. Most of the time, however, the river is low enough to prevent these adventurers. And when it's really high and rushing; i.e., when the Ministry of Natural resources has removed a few logs from the log chute bridge to increase the flow – there is always the bridge just below us to prevent motorized vehicles from chugging upstream. For the Little Kennisis is part of the Trent-Severn Waterway, a controlled river providing water to the locks of that system to the south of us. One of the advantages of that is, for canoeists and lately kayakers, a long trip can take you down our river and through the systems of connected rivers and lakes right to the waterway itself.

Still, the magic? Here are some astounding experiences of living on the Little Kennisis River. Every spring there are pairs of nesting ducks – wood ducks, black ducks, mergansers and American mergansers in their snow white feathers, buffleheads – who mate and raise their young on our river. We hear the mating loudly on spring evenings, as we hear the frogs – heralds of environmental health – praising and welcoming spring. We also have a pair of American Bitterns nesting close to where we live, and a variety of hawks soaring overhead. Grouse, wild turkeys in their dozens, owls of many varieties make the forests home. One spring we encountered a nesting loon, right on the river's edge, who grew accustomed to our reassuring voices every day. So accustomed, that when the two babies were born and she took them out on the water, she allowed us to come within a few feet of them without diving away. Seeing mink, beaver and otter, weasel, fox and fisher is an everyday occurrence. Deer come to drink, and bear cross the river frequently in their active seasons. Recently we had cougar sightings – a young male, seven feet long – before the MNR tagged and removed him to a more northern location. Most of these sightings occur when you are here for a long period of time, not occasional visits. We know enough to respect their ownership of this land and have never had a problem with any wild animal.

In this technological age, is this not magic enough – to dwell in peace, season after season, with these creatures who share their land with us, and grace us with their presence? Some days we are breathless with the privilege of living thus in the magic of life on the Little Kennisis River.

*published previously in "Sideroads of Haliburton", 2008*

# A Park For All Seasons: Stanhope Township's

## Elvin Johnson Park*

Tucked away at the end of a "no exit" road on the northern edge of Halls Lake in the Alquonquin Highlands is a corner of heaven on a warm summer day. If you come north on Highway 35 from Carnarvon, make a right onto Little Hawk Lake Road (just a little way past Halls Lake Market, the finest bakery around), and drive for three kilometers, you will come to a junction. On the left is Big Hawk Lake Rd, leading to the historic log chute and a marina for the water access only cottages on Big Hawk Lake. But on the right, just a few feet further than the sign pole, is Old Mill Road, signless except for its name, which leads to The Elvin Johnson Park, the name of which doesn't appear on any sign.

So who was Elvin Johnson? And how did he come to merit this little gem of a park being named after him? He was born at Halls Lake in 1914, and spent most of his life in Stanhope township, becoming one of the founding fathers of Stanhope. (He is quoted as having said that "one month in Toronto" was enough for him.) Without him this small patch of land – boasting more lakes than any other township in Haliburton County – might have faded away with the logging industry. Farming on Boshkung Lake as a young adult with his Jersey Islands wife Ruby, without water or electricity or a car – just a team of horses, Johnson was a pioneer in the true sense of that word. They raised Muscovi ducks, chickens, pigs, and always a team of horses, though there was no real road at that time, just a dirt track. By the 1930's, Johnson needed more to support his growing family, so he became involved in surveying land between Twelve Mile Lake and Dorset for the "new road" : Highway 35. With no real tools except by hand, blasting through the rock faces was – by our standards – Herculean.

Here are some of the community contributions Elvin Johnson made in his lifetime: he served on the School Committee, the Dump Committee, the Roads Committee, the Board of Management, the Community Centre Committee, and the Parks and Recreation Committee – all of them collaborating to make Stanhope a viable township within the county. He was Commissioner of the (first) Telephone System when five or six homes were connected to the one party line. He also spent sixteen years through several terms as a councilor, and was Deputy Reeve from 1985-1988. In the early 70's, he was responsible for creating the Stanhope Fire Department against strong belief that the township couldn't support such a venture. The first pumper arrived in 1973 - and twenty men volunteered. During those years he also was a leader in rebuilding the Hawk Lake Log Chute on the Kennisis River through a Federally sponsored Winter Works project in 1971 – in the depth of winter. Here was a strong man with other strong men.

The Elvin Johnson Park is perhaps the clearest recognition of Johnson's contribution to the Stanhope community, and one that carries his name into the present and the future. While he was on council, the MNR offered this land to the township to develop into a park, but no one seemed interested, so Johnson took it on himself, with the council's encouragement. It took him a couple of years to complete the park with the help of students, and in 1988, at the age of 74 – when he announced that he wasn't going to run for council again – he received the offer of having the park named after him. That same year, he received the honor of "Stanhope Citizen of the Year."**

Could there be a better example of community-mindedness, of a life given in service, hard steady work, creativity and thoughtfulness – not only for people, but for this land around us, which supports us every day? The park commemorates this life, and offers us a glimpse into a past not so distant in years, but definitely distant in values and the giving of talent, strength and self for one's community. Such was Elvin Johnson, and he deserves commemoration in this public way.

So – with that history – what can you expect at The Elvin Johnson Park? It is a water's edge delight of nature. Located at the northern edge of Halls Lake, just to the right of where the Little Kennisis River runs into the lake, the little park produces a variety of possibilities for families, picnics and solitary readers and writers. It's sandy beach extends for several meters out from the shore, making water play safe for little ones just getting to know themselves in water, and inviting for longer range, experienced swimmers. In fact, most weekday mornings in the summer, the township provides swimming lessons for children of all ages. Picnic tables, sheltered and unsheltered, washrooms, a small playground and fireplaces provide welcoming focal points for people of all ages to gather.

Besides the forest surrounding the park, trees provide shade along some of the shoreline. At the far left corner, facing the water, you can even walk around to a private, sheltered cove which most people never discover. It is dotted with driftwood and weathered roots, and offers an even deeper quiet than the park itself. Readers and writers attend!

To the right of the beach is a narrow causeway, just enough for one car at a time, going over to the lake's island where several lucky people own summer cottages with stupendous views around the island's rocky edges. The causeway sports a boat launch also. Fishing boats quietly dot the water, especially in early morning.

One night a week for the summer months, Stanhope Township offers a campfire with a variety of themes in Elvin Johnson Park. These can be anything from "Scary Stories", Traditional Singalongs, looking at the night sky with an astronomer, visits from an old logger – and every year there are new themes. A Google search will quickly bring you the list for the coming summer.

Each morning in every season, when my companion and I, with our Golden Retriever Kai, walk along Old Mill Road to the park, we encounter some form of wild life. Deer roam the forest. Arctic hare zig-zag back and forth across our path almost every day, white in winter, brown in summer. Their sole purpose seems to be to taunt the dog, for they wait in complete stillness until we are almost there; then they run across in front of us. Grouse waddle slowly across the road. In spring and summer we shoo the occasional black bear back into the woods. Merlin Falcons screech at crows and ravens, claiming their territory, and in June we've watched them loudly teach their chicks to fly. Song sparrows, mourning doves, white-throated sparrows, woodpeckers – pileated, hairy and downy – a few owls – weave the walk with sound. A final reward, reaching Elvin Johnson Park, is hearing the long, slow loon call fill the air, for a pair of loons still returns to Halls Lake every summer. We take it as a sign that – despite the cottages and their loud water toys – Halls Lake can still sustain a nesting pair, when other lakes in our area cannot.

In autumn, Elvin Johnson Park takes on a different and more haunting beauty. the swimming docks are pulled onshore, the park usually deserted, when the mists of the lake make their mysterious appearance, morning after morning. The park becomes like an outdoor auditorium, a place to sit or stand while watching the mists move and shift, fade, disappear and reveal colors more vivid as fall deepens. If slowing down is what you want to do, mist-watching in autumn in Elvin Johnson Park is a sure investment of time and attention.

Thank you, Elvin Johnson. Your park continues to be a well-cared for corner of the Alquonquin Highlands. It's worth looking for, especially on those summer days when sitting next to water is necessary, or when the mists of autumn stop your breath with beauty.

*\*published previously in "Sideroads of Haliburton", February 2009*
*\*\*information from Supplement to The Times, Minden, July 22, 1991*

# Circuit of Five Viewpoints (CFV) Hiking Trail
(previously published in "Sideroads of Haliburton", April 2009)

Circuit of Five Viewpoints: now isn't that an interesting name for a trail? And the history of this hiking trail is just as interesting, just as layered, in how the stunning panoramas of the Five Viewpoints came to be melded into one very inviting hike on a cool autumn day – or at any time of year, really. We have even walked this trail on snowshoes in mid-winter.

The seeds of a trail dream had their beginnings when the James Cooper trail on the North Shore Road was donated to Stanhope Township. Then, in the year 2000, the old Alvin Ferguson ski trail was linked to the James Cooper Trail to make a hiking trail, but a shorter one. The year 2001 saw these two opening to a newly carved out trail going several kilometers north towards Little Hawk Lake, and the first hike on the old Ridge Trail close to Little Hawk Lake Road took place in 2002. A Trail Head for CFV was established at the parking lot for Little Hawk Lake itself. Not much later, when Dan and Dawn Muir allowed the extension of the trail to include the Crests of the Kennisis viewpoint which borders on their property, the complete circuit could be completed, and the Crests of the Kennisis Trail was opened as the final piece of this magnificent walk. Good boots are recommended.

Who, you might ask, would have such a vision of the possibilities for this near wildness, the hills and valleys overgrown and thick with forest? And who would then undertake the daunting task and significant time needed to carve these trails through the bush? Those of us who so love and use the CFV trail owe our deep gratitude to Peter and Margaret Brogden, Keith and Mary Waggett and Stu Bain, who together undertook to open and maintain these trails. Peter is the source of this history, and – sadly – also pointed out to me that the Memorial Bench overlooking the Crests of the Kennissis is in memory of Keith Waggett and Stu Bain, both of whom have passed away since the task was completed.

And now for the experience. In the summer that I moved to Halls Lake, 2003, this trail system had its formal opening at the trail head close to Little Hawk Lake. Though this happened only a couple of weeks after the move, and surrounded by boxes as we were, I was drawn to attend, having read the announcement in the *Minden Times*.

A small group was gathered – now I know that perhaps most were the people named above – and a few stragglers like myself who love hiking and were excited by the opening of a new trail. Declaring the trails open was no less solemn a moment, and we set off up to the top of the rock face with a peculiar freedom and joy and perhaps some awe at the accomplishment.

Since that time, the whole trail has become familiar to me. One Thanksgiving weekend we began at the North Shore Road and took about five hours, meandering, eating, photographing and examining everything in fine detail, to reach the Little Hawk Trail Head. The variations of the trails mean that they are never boring: up hill and down dale, surrounded by a rich plethora of growth that varies with every kilometer. It's a nature photographer's paradise, no matter what the season.

Three years ago, after the tornado passed though the Halls/Little Hawk Lakes area, the hiking trail was devastated. Tall pines were pitched around like pick-up sticks, making many parts of the trail impassable. Since we live close to the trail, we biked to it every day, going as far as we could. Amazingly, within three or four days, the trail was mostly cleared and definitely passable. The dedication of Peter and company was wondrous. To the sides of the trail, however, even today, you can see the blow-down caused by the tornado still quite visible even after these intervening years. Seeing it causes the imagination to picture the devastation that was visible the day after – it was considerable.

Having the Circuit of Five Viewpoints Trail within walking distance of where we live is an unexpected bonus of living on the Little Kennissis River. There are so many variations to be explored, and short or long hikes to suit your schedule, that only in the deep snow and cold of late January and February would we consider not going. The trail is a staple activity for every other season of the year.

From an entrance close to the Hawk Lake Landfill, you can climb to one of the viewpoints in about 20 minutes, surveying Halls Lake and all the surrounding countryside. Just below you the Little Kennissis winds through trees and marshes. In autumn it is wordlessly beautiful, but equally so in other seasons, I have discovered. Or – if you begin at the Historic Log Chute, in about two hours you'll reach the lookout mentioned above. That two hours is to me the most stupendous part of the trail, and perhaps the most strenuous. Called "Crests of the Kennissis", it takes the hiker up and down, along gigantic outcroppings of granite, multiple caves, dripping moss, rainforest shade, resting places many and needed. The silence that only deep forest contains is prevalent in these rich valleys, while the high lookout points give miles of vision and whatever winds prevail. Good binoculars definitely add to the experience of these vistas, and you might be amazed at what you can see. Or you can enter along a skidoo trail, through the gravel pits from Braeloch road, and climb quickly to see another panorama altogether, and continue for a different two hours, again rising and falling with the land, until you come out close to the Trail Head at little Hawk Lake.

A good map of the whole system is available from the Trails and Tours office in Carnarvon. And the whole or parts of this Hiking Trail will be offered for guided hikes in the Hike Haliburton Festival during the weekend of October 17-19, 2008.

Leave your usual world behind for an hour or two and treat yourself to the banquet of nature that awaits you anywhere along the Circuit of Five Viewpoints Hiking Trail. Come north from Carnarvon on Highway 35 and turn right onto Little Hawk Lake Road until you come to the Trail Head at the Lake itself. Or start at the North Shore Road and end at one of the viewpoints (a car at both ends would help.) These trails await with wonder and variety and spectacular scenery.

# Found: Kai's Amazing Adventure*

The story of Kai, the lost and found Golden Retriever of Halls Lake, begins with a bear and ends with a bear. Here's how it happened.

On Saturday morning, June 24, Joan Weir – Kai's companion person – took Kai for their usual early morning outing along Old Mill Rd. Joan was riding her bike, an occasional way to give Kai a good run. Just as they were turning the last corner onto Little Hawk Lake Rd., they startled and were startled by a bear that was in the bush to their left, close to the road. The bear swiftly climbed the nearest tree, making much noise and fuss.

Kai was so spooked that she wrenched the plastic handle of the extendible leash out of Joan's hand and headed for home. Even though Joan was on a bike, she couldn't keep up with Kai, who reached the back door only a few seconds before her, with the plastic handle dragging on the road behind her, making a fearsome noise and continuing Kai's fright. When the door wasn't open, Kai kept going, though Joan wasn't fast enough to see in what direction she had gone, leash and all.

Then began the search. Joan's neighbor Rick suspended his morning plans and searched with her. They scoured the woods in all directions for hours without seeing a trace of her. When Rick had to go, several of Joan's friends from the area, and one from Orillia, took up the search. They came and stayed, in shifts and whenever they could. They brought food and stayed the night. They went out in rain in the dark. They made posters, placed them everywhere, and knocked on doors with Joan.

The searching went on for four nights and four and a half days. By this time the whole neighborhood knew that Kai was missing. Joan

107

realized that she had gone into thick bush with a leash and was tangled somewhere, but where? She called two animal communicators who both told her that Kai was alive, and even described the spot where she was, but couldn't say exactly where that spot might be in relation to the house. Joan's housemate Brenda was teaching in Ireland at the time, and calling two and three times a day for support, as well as communing with Kai herself, reassuring her and encouraging her to chew the leash, which she didn't do. When Joan announced the dilemma on the Golden Rescue website, twenty-two people from different parts of Ontario offered to come and search if she wasn't found by Friday of that week.

Finally, on Wednesday, June 28 a phone call came. Pat Allingham was visiting her daughter Samantha, who was working for the summer at Little Hawk Resort. On her way to the house where Samantha was staying, she was driving past the Hawk Lake Landfill when she spotted a small bear cub in the greenery of the hydro line, just across from the landfill. She stopped to look, and suddenly Kai's golden head popped up from the grasses, not a foot away from the bear cub. Pat went on to Samantha's and said "I believe I just saw the lost dog" and called Joan right away. Luckily, she also went back to the site, freed Kai from her leash, and Joan arrived just afterwards, falling to her knees in joy and hysterical relief.

It began with a bear, and it ended with a bear.

But there are other dimensions to this story.

Joan had hardly slept or eaten since it began. She wrestled the entire time with her fears and possible loss. On the morning that Kai was found, Joan had a dream that Kai was alive, and with bears, though unharmed. Meanwhile, Brenda, in Ireland, while receiving an energy treatment on the Monday morning, kept hearing the word "found" all through the treatment. But what was particularly stunning and overwhelming for Joan was the magnificent generosity of people who gave their time, their resources, their food, their company. Their readiness to give up personal plans in order to search again and again was magnanimous, was "the extra mile." And the fact that strangers from all over Ontario from the Golden Rescue group were willing to come and search for Kai on the Friday of the holiday weekend was a testimony to how many good-hearted people there really are in the world. This is the kind of story seldom heard and that is why we want to tell it.

Except for a small gash on one front paw, Kai was completely unharmed, though she had lost seven pounds. All that time she had been in an area populated by 25-30 bears, very near the landfill. There are also wolves and coyotes, foxes and fishers in this area. But Kai had come to no harm whatsoever. Now she is a little skittish when we walk past the spot where the bear was just as frightened as she was, but there seem to be no other repercussions from her ordeal. What an important lesson for all of us who project our own fears onto animals, who – after all and rightfully so given the way we treat them – want to stay as far away from us humans as they can. While we always need to be cautious and respectful of all the animals in the woods, it is so unfair and inappropriate of us to see them as ready to attack us at a moments notice.

Now that Kai is back and safe, we joke and say that perhaps she wanted a fasting vision quest!

*previously published in The Minden Times, 31 July, 2006*

# Kentucky Fried Christmas*

There are some people who say that Christmas has no magic. I know otherwise. Christmas magic is a shred of shining delight in an unexpected gift, and that's what this story is about. It's also a true story, and happened just last year, and I'm still being surprised and delighted by it.

Last year in early December I arranged to meet an old friend in Toronto for a few days. I see this friend only once or twice a year, so when we get together, there is a lot of catching up to be done, usually over wine and good meals, accompanied by poetry and book sharing. We made the best of being in downtown Toronto in the early Christmas season, eating out and wandering the snowy streets, doing useless things like visiting the Bata Shoe Museum and commenting on the decorations along Bloor West, as well as visiting bookstores and the ROM. Enough to clear one's mind of daily tasks and usual obligations.

It was a leisurely, lovely visit with a Christmas aura around it, and when I drove her to Union Station to get the train back to London, I was feeling full and grateful for the people in my life with whom I share a common language and a long history. I remember thinking this thought as I drove west on Bloor, facing a sunset of soft pink light that makes even crowded city scenes more than tolerable. In the midst of this grateful glow, I suddenly wanted some Kentucky Fried Chicken.

Now anyone who knows me would stare in wonder at this news. I can hardly tolerate fast food of any kind, and Kentucky Fried chicken is close to the top of that list. Into my mind came the phrase "boneless wings:" I'd heard them advertised many times and idly wondered what they might be like; now they attacked me with acute desire. I decided to look for the nearest KFC, all the while with another part of me standing aside and saying "what's going on?" I drove along Bloor West to no avail; close to the Jane St. intersection I decided to ask someone where the nearest KFC was. There was a parking space and I pulled into it smoothly. Everything was conspiring, it seemed, to get me to a Kentucky Fried Chicken store at 5 o'clock on a glowing December evening in a crowded city. I went into a dollar store and asked the clerk: sure enough, directions were clear and precise and directed me to turn the corner onto Jane St. and go two blocks to Dundas, and there it was on the south corner.

Still amazed at this sudden direction my life had taken in a few seconds, I nevertheless pulled into the parking lot. By now it was dark, and through the store's window I could see a long, ragged line of people hoping for chicken: it was, after all, now 5:30 pm. I was able to park close to the store lights, and as I got out of the car, two tall and burly men, in their late twenties or early thirties, approached me. My heart skipped a beat – all senses went on high alert. One said "Ma'am, we're really hungry and have no money – please, would you be able to get us a piece of chicken?"

Now to me these men looked ordinarily dressed and not at all noticeably poor. Once I gained my inner ground again, I realized that the whiff of alcohol was in the air, and I knew then why they had no money. Berating refusals began to form in my mind. Then a strange thing happened. It was as if some sweeping wind cleared away all fear and a judgment that I suddenly saw I had no right to be making, and I said "OK – go over there to the side of the building and wait for me. I'll bring you out a piece of chicken."

In I go to stand in the long impatient line of tired customers. While waiting, my rational mind starts arguing again. "What are you doing, giving food to drunks? They might attack you" and other such torments whirled around in my puzzled mind. But there was something bigger, something soft and tender, something compassionate and beyond reason wrapping my little rational mind in cotton wool, full as a Christmas stocking. I was feeling my own gratitude too fully for such narrow thinking to have sway, and while in the line I thought "Those men need more than a piece of chicken."

So when I finally got to the ordering place, my first request was for them: "what's the biggest meal you offer?" I said. "Three pieces of chicken, large fries, cole slaw, and cookie with a large drink," was the reply. "Give me two," I said and a small order of boneless wings" – the wings, at least, hadn't gotten lost in ordering large dinners.

Once or twice during the wait, I glimpsed the men peeking through the window to see where I was in the line, and my only thought was – they must be mighty hungry.

When I finally received and paid for everything, I was walking out the door with two large bags and a tiny order of boneless wings that fit in the palm of one hand. The men were waiting for me. "I'm sorry it took so long, I said." (My other mind was saying "are you crazy?") They were immediately bowing – they might have been Eastern European – and said "Ma'am, you shouldn't be apologizing to us – and look what you've bought us! O Ma'am, thank you, thank you so much, we are so hungry…" and off they went with the bags around the dark corner of the KFC building.

Slowly I opened my car door and got in. So that was what the Kentucky Fried Chicken impulse was about, I thought. Those men needed food, and somehow I was led there to provide it. Who knows why, in that large, incomprehensible tapestry of light we call the world? As I pulled away, turning back Jane St. to the Bloor West intersection, I felt that shining sliver of another world breaking through into my small, narrow-minded judgmental one. Perhaps my own full and grateful heart for all I'd been receiving for two days, and the abundance of my own life here in Haliburton and in many parts of the world, opened some inner door to another way of seeing. I gave those men a chicken dinner, but their gift to me was by far the greatest and the longest lasting. That was the real surprise. Their gift was this: countless times since that day, I have experienced my logical, rational mind urging me into small-mindedness, anxiety and fear. The gift of this encounter returns again and again to show me that the opening of my compassionate heart, even when the narrow mind is screaming and bullying, expands me into grace and light. And it didn't even happen on Christmas itself. I believe there is a song about that: "and what if every day were like Christmas?"

There are some people who say that Christmas has no magic. I surely know otherwise. That glow of my Kentucky Fried Christmas still gives me light.

*previously published in The Haliburton Echo Christmas Supplement, 2009*

# The Christmas Midwives*
(previously published in the
Haliburton Echo Christmas Supplement, 2008)

When our neighbor asked if we would tend to his dog for a few days during Christmas while his family attended a reunion, he assured us that – though she was visibly carrying puppies – she wouldn't give birth until a few days after he was due to return.

This was our first Christmas in the Alquonquin Highlands. Joan and I had moved from Etobicoke at July's end to a treed property right on the edge of the Little Kennisis River. We thought we were in heaven, even in the damp, mosquito-filled summer of that year. And we continued to think so, even as we learned that not everything in the house was as sound as we had thought, even when the wood we had arranged to be delivered was too wet and too big, and even when we learned that wood heat is an art as well as a science.

So we were welcoming the approach of Christmas as a bit of a break, and Joan in particular, being the dog-lover, was more than fine with attending to our neighbor's dog from Christmas Eve morning until December 29. So – on Christmas Eve in the late afternoon – we both went to take the eight-year-old retriever for a walk. I noticed at that time that her belly was very low, almost touching the ground, and I pointed this out to Joan. The first buzz of anxiety began its hum deep inside me. Later that night, after our gift-opening and Christmas Eve dinner (something told us to do it that evening instead of next morning), Joan went to take the dog for another walk. When she returned, she shook

114

her head with worry. "I don't know about this," she said, "I don't know how she can last for another five days."

About four o'clock on Christmas morning, Joan shook me awake. It was very dark. "I can't get her out of my mind," she said. "I'm going up now, and if anything is happening I'll call you. Can you come now if there is?" I agreed to get up and get to the house if I was needed, and off she went into the Christmas morning darkness, a crisp starry sky overhead. Afterwards I remarked that birth was in the air. Isn't that the meaning of Christmas anyway? There wasn't long to wait. My phone rang. "Come as quick as you can," said Joan's anxious voice, "she's already had four puppies, and she's in distress."

I dressed with closed eyes and made my sleepy way over the icy driveway, falling only once. Already the winter was a freeze-and-thaw affair that made walking treacherous, and I hadn't developed rural walking skills yet. When I arrived, so had two more puppies. We were up to six. Mama was showing signs of fatigue; she had already birthed a litter of ten six months before. There was no way that we could – or would even think of – leaving her. We settled in. As each slick and shiny coal-black puppy emerged in its tight little sack, we never once tired of watching the amazing instinct of the mother, who licked off the sack and kept licking the chest until the puppy began to breathe. Then we placed the puppy at a nipple and watched life make its milky beginning.

Before 11 am on Christmas morning, twelve puppies had been born. Joan, who has medical training, helped remove the last four. As each one was born, we gave him or her a Christmas name; "Holly," "Ivy," "Shepherd," "Nicky," "Noel," for starters. Twelve taxed our Christmas vocabulary of names. The last puppy born, the tiniest of all and needing the most help, was eventually the only one kept by the owners and named – of course – "Angel."

Throughout Christmas morning, we kept calling our neighbor and saying "Now you have six!" and "now you have nine!" We were all very relieved to say that number twelve was the last. Then came the cleanup.

Throughout the whole of Christmas Day and for the next three days, Joan and I took turns attending to the thirteen dogs. Sometimes one of us would take Mama for a walk while the other stayed with the puppies. They were all, without exception or a single mark, black and shiny – the border-collie Dad's influence- though the Mother was a rich-red burnished Golden Retriever. Because they were all so alike, it was difficult to keep track of them, so we ended up having to count twelve several times a day. We also helped the smaller ones get a turn at one of Mama's nipples, since the sizes varied considerably and the bigger ones tended to get to nipples first and hang on. In this way, all twelve lived with considerable vitality.

Early in the cleanup process I went alone to remove the soiled blankets on which the birth had taken place. After I had put down fresh blankets, meanwhile putting all the puppies into a basket for easy counting, I began to place them back onto the Mother's nipples. There were only eleven. Back to the basket. Only eleven. I frantically tore apart the old blankets, now in a green garbage bag, and soon heard the little mewing. My heart pounding with relief, I got the tiny black ball of fur back to a nipple as quickly as I could, pushing two bigger puppies out of the way for the moment.

Within a few days, the whole neighborhood knew the story of the Christmas puppies and began calling Joan and myself "the midwives of Halls Lake." This title followed us for a long time, certainly until every puppy had gone to a home that wanted him or her. Most days of that winter we visited those puppies in the pen our neighbor had made for them. We cuddled them and watched them grow and eventually laughed as they undid our boot laces and crawled up our legs. Our neighbor had no trouble at all finding homes for every one of them. His care for them was stellar.

As for Joan and me, the "Christmas Midwives," we felt as if we'd been given a great gift, that Christmas. Yes, we had plans – the usual plans for Christmas – food and visiting and presents. But in the midst of that most predictable of holidays, a window into heaven had opened up and invited us to step through. The messiness of life, which culminates in birth of whatever kind, paid us a visit, and opened its starry heart to the truest meaning of Christmas we could ever encounter. What could be better than being present at a birth on Christmas morning, Mother and puppies equally vulnerable? Because that's where all of it – every little thing we love and treasure and avoid and dismiss – that's where everything begins again.